Lost Boys of Hannibal

John Wingate

Wisdom Editions

Minneapolis, Minnesota

Wisdom
Editions

Minneapolis

FIRST EDITION DECEMBER 2017

Printed in the United States of America.

10 9 8 7 6 5 4 3 2 1

Cover and interior design: Gary Lindberg

ISBN: 978-1-939548-80-1

Dedicated with love and gratitude to Lynae, Annya, Amelia, my mother Betty, and siblings Sharon and Brad. In remembrance of my father, Bud, who always taught us to do our best and to persevere in worthy endeavors.

Table of Contents

Introduction   1

Chapter 1: The Last Day   11

Chapter 2: Calamity at Nightfall   27

Chapter 3: Other Lost Children   39

Chapter 4: Running Out of Time   61

Chapter 5: "They're Below Us:"   98

Chapter 6: "We Have Blood Here!"   119

Chapter 7: Missouri - the Cave State   147

Chapter 8: Growing Despair, A Mother's Plea   165

Chapter 9: Bill Karras, Controversial Caver   189

Chapter 10: Bodies in the Basement?   211

Chapter 11: Underground Again, Renewed Hope   219

Chapter 12: Boys and Risk   223

Chapter 13: A Vexing Mystery   227

Postscript: Two More Theories   239

Resources   245

Acknowledgements

Someone once said the hardest part of writing a book is putting one word after another. Humor is a great way to describe a complex process. Years in development, this journalistic account was challenging, tracking down key players after half a century and hoping their memories were fresh and intact. But everyone rose to the occasion and shared to the best of their recollections. The list of those to thank is a long one: the cavers, the family members, and friends who were gracious in allowing me to listen as we discussed a painful time in their lives. You have my heartfelt thanks for helping tell the story so the lost boys and the heroic responders are honored and remembered.

A special thanks to the late Jerry Vineyard, Missouri's Deputy State Geologist and cave expert, who graciously shared his expertise and personal stories of the search effort. Thanks to the members of the caving grottos in Missouri and Illinois who contributed their heroic service, personal reflections and important background to help a non-caver better understand the Hannibal search and all of the associated search dynamics surrounding the crisis.

My thanks and gratitude to the Hannibal Courier-Post and its editor Eric Dundon, the Quincy Herald-Whig and photo editor Joe Liesen, the Hannibal Public Library, Dan Bledsoe, Brad Wingate, Annya Wingate, Susan Baker, David Mahon and Dwight Weaver for providing photographs seen in these pages. Special thanks to Howard Hoffmaster who served as editor of the Hannibal Courier Post in 1967. Now retired, he demonstrated a remarkable memory and a faithful adherence to fact when interviewed. The narrative for this book, about an event so long ago, necessarily relied upon use of newspaper clippings to supplement personal interviews and the extensive research necessary to develop timelines and the overall story.

Staff of the Missouri Department of Natural Resources, the Missouri Department of Transportation, and the Missouri Speleological Society were gracious to share their comments and photographs regarding the 2006 cave discovery at the construction site for the new Stowell Elementary School.

Special thanks to the late William Karras, Conway Christiansen, Woody St. Clair, Fred Hoag, Lynnie Hoag-Pedigo, Gary Rush, Ed Owen, Ron Owen, Bill Owen, Steve Sederwall, Ruth Martin Ellison, Richard Ellison, Joyce Sorrell Gonzales, Alfred King, John Janes, Dr. Stan Sides, Don Nicholson, Jim Mrozkowski, Jim Arrigo, Bob Cowder, John Hemple, John Lyng, Joe Liesen, Kong, Charles Webster, Bob Cowder, Dwight Weaver, Joe Walsh, Jim Rodemaker, David Mahon, National Speleological Society Historian Gary Soule, speleohistorians Jack Speece and Jo Schaper, Col. Bill Tucker, Louise Kohler, Joe Tripodi, Ann Schallert, Mike Morgan, Brian Borton, Susan Baker, Karen Townes, Amanda Keefe, Milton Martin, Bill Boltinghouse, Wesley Tischer, Al Viar, Jeff Crews, R. Scott House, Kenneth Grush, Don Dunham, Dan Lamping, William Pfantz, Dave Bunnell, Bill Torode, Carol Tiderman, Rich Wolfert, Don Rimbach, Linda Coleberd, and many others. I'm grateful for your expertise, recollections and support in honoring the lost boys and all those brave and dedicated men and women who selflessly gave of themselves during the historic crisis. Finally, thank you to my publishers, Gary Lindberg and Ian Leask of Calumet Editions, and their editor, Rick Polad.

Lost Boys of Hannibal

John Wingate

Aerial view of historic Hannibal, Missouri. The wooded hill, lower center right, is the location of Murphy's Cave and other smaller maze caves searched in 1967. Photo courtesy George E. Walley, Jr. 2010.

Introduction

Historic Hannibal, Missouri sits nestled in a gentle curve of the Mississippi River, about one hundred nautical miles north of St. Louis and seventeen miles downstream from Quincy, Illinois. It is a river town that even today draws largely on Mark Twain's literary legacy for its dominant industry—tourism.

Hannibal was briefly the boyhood home of Samuel Clemens during the 1840s. But Clemens, who used Mark Twain as a literary pen name, lived there long enough for civic leaders to permanently embrace the great American author and proclaim Hannibal as *America's Hometown.*

After crossing the Mississippi River from Illinois and approaching the town on the Mark Twain Memorial Bridge, 1960s visitors were greeted with a barrage of visual cues that left little uncertainty about their destination: Mark Twain Dinette, Becky Thatcher Restaurant, Steamboat Realty, Huck Finn Cinema. Switch on the radio and a local FM station's promotional jingle proclaimed the region as "Great River Country."

For decades, much of the prosperity here has been tied to the past. Old brick buildings that once served as houses of ill repute during the nineteenth century, doing a booming human trade with visiting riverboat hands, later evolved into quaint tourist haunts. Antique, book and gift shops, craft stores, several restaurants, and the Mark Twain boyhood home and museum, along with other historic landmarks, can be found in the historic Main Street district that hugs the riverfront.

From May through October, tourists from around the world spill into town to experience a bit of Mark Twain's history. During the 1960s, the *Hannibal Courier-Post* newspaper's front page listed the hometowns of visitors who had journeyed the greatest distances to visit Hannibal. Typically, the visitors usually hailed from the Far East, Europe, Australia, Africa, and all fifty US states.

They came to Hannibal to sample a unique bit of classic Americana, to see firsthand the landmarks they'd read about in the pages of Twain's classics. If asked, most would agree that idyllic Hannibal with its historic Cardiff Hill Lighthouse, Mark Twain Cave, cobblestone riverfront and historic Victorian homes seemed like a great place to call America's hometown.

Hannibal was a popular 1960's destination for station-wagoned families, the great sights and venues easily enjoyed over a relaxing long weekend.

Several times during those steamy summer days, visitors heard the dissonant calliope of a tourist riverboat making its way downstream to a riverfront berth just a few blocks beyond Mark Twain's whitewashed boyhood home.

The words of Twain and the adventurous spirit he breathed into characters like Tom Sawyer, Huckleberry Finn, and Becky Thatcher remain enmeshed in the fabric of life in this old river town. Cardiff Hill, with its historic lighthouse, was named by Twain himself after one of his favorite places in Wales. Twain used the locale as a popular haunt for Tom and Huck as they found adventure and trouble.

For children growing up in Hannibal, the exploration of the wooded hills has always come naturally, true to the tradition of Tom, Huck and Becky. Playing among the wooded river bluffs overlooking the half-mile-wide Mississippi, boys and girls became explorers in search of Indians, river pirates or whatever foe happened to challenge the imagination on a carefree summer day.

And then, there are the caves.

It is no coincidence that Missouri is called the Cave State. It has more caves than most other states (7,300 and counting), the vast majority of these having been discovered since the 1950s. The geology of northeast Missouri is distinctive with a layer of Louisiana Lithographic Limestone, up to sixty feet thick in places, within the hills and bluffs. In this massive stratum of limestone are intricate systems of complex maze caves and labyrinths of smaller caves created by the waters of an ancient sea percolating through cracks in the limestone over a span of millions of years.

These caves exist in an area roughly one mile wide by three miles long, from Bear Creek in the city limits southward. Perhaps at one time, the several large maze caves within this area comprised one massive and continuous subterranean maze system.

Then, about half a million years ago, the northern third of Missouri was heavily affected by glaciers as the ice and rock sculpted the land, cutting through the hills and cave system and creating the valleys we see today. Now, these maze caves appear as separate and distinctive karst environments, but their closed off passages suggest a larger, intact cave system carved out eons ago.

It's believed the steep, high bluffs, known as the Lincoln Hills, along the Mississippi River near Hannibal largely escaped glaciation. Today, the rugged bluffs and exposed bedrock cliff faces comprise the steep topography that makes driving Northeast Missouri such a scenic endeavor.

One of the most famous maze caverns in the nation, and Missouri's first show cave, is Mark Twain Cave, located a mile south of Hannibal and a few hundred yards west of State Highway 79. The cave served as an important literary setting as Tom and Becky hid from Injun Joe, and it remains a wildly popular tourist destination today.

In The Adventures of Tom Sawyer, Twain wrote:

> No man knew the cave; that it was an impossible thing. Most of the young men knew a portion of it, and it was not customary to venture beyond the known portion. Tom Sawyer knew as much of the cave as anyone.

In fiction, as in real life, the cave has always been a source of mystery, adventure, and angst. Today, Mark Twain Cave and nearby

Cameron Cave are safe, well-managed tourist attractions providing visitors with an opportunity to vicariously experience the flavor of Twain's enduring fictional tales.

One of the attention-getting highlights of a Mark Twain Cave tour comes as the experienced guide, self-assured with powerful flashlight in hand, turns off the electric lights that illuminate the narrow, damp and stony passageways—the only route back out. The smothering, inky darkness settles around you, reinforcing the futility of escape without light. A cave tourist literally cannot see a hand held in front of their face.

The "lights off" novelty, a part of every cave tour, generates nervous laughter among cave visitors and offers a subtle reminder of the dangers of this subterranean world and how quickly exploration might turn tragic for the ill-prepared. The imagination quickly responds, and anxiety rises. Visitors recognize how easily one could face great peril if lost without light and provisions, perhaps to stumble, break a limb and slowly succumb in the damp fifty-two-degree chill. After the tour, everyone is relieved to bask in the comforting, warming rays of the summer sun once again.

Growing up in Hannibal and exploring the numerous caves, rocky bluffs, the nooks and crannies of the hilly terrain, has been a youthful ritual for generations of children. Scrambling through rock quarries, forests, and along sheer limestone bluffs overlooking the Mississippi, one might find musket balls from the civil war era, arrowheads from early Indian settlements, and plenty of reasons to be late for supper on warm evenings when the lure of adventure beckoned youthful explorers to stay a while longer.

***

Joel Hoag   Billy Hoag   Craig Dowell

Lost Boys of Hannibal is the story of three boys who shared a deep sense of adventure and a mysterious fate. Joel (Joey) Hoag, thirteen, his brother (William) Billy Hoag, eleven, and their neighbor (Edwin) Craig Dowell, fourteen, loved to explore. These modern-day Twain characters hiked the hilly neighborhoods of Hannibal's Southside, explored the cave passages, some long-known and others more recently revealed by State Highway 79 road construction near their homes. They had great fun exploring this dark underworld until one evening in May 1967 when they never came home.

In their search for adventure, the trio ultimately met a tragic fate which propelled Hannibal—*America's Hometown*—into headlines around the world.

How could three boys simply vanish after school on a sun-splashed afternoon? Were they trapped and killed by a cave collapse while exploring? Were they victims of abduction and foul play? Is it possible that they ran away? Even today, these questions linger in the minds of the family members, friends, and townspeople who can never forget what happened half a century ago.

The focus of the search was Murphy's Cave, a Southside cave first identified nearly one hundred years earlier, and a State Highway 79 construction site a few blocks from the boys' homes. State Highway 79 was being rerouted and widened as a scenic roadway from Hannibal to St. Louis, one that offered sweeping views of the Mississippi and the steep hills and valleys of northeastern Missouri.

Construction workers dynamited and moved millions of tons of rock and earth as they cut a swath through a forested, rocky hill, atop which is Lover's Leap, the popular scenic overlook which endures. The entire Cypress Street neighborhood was taken as the highway crews' earthmovers resculpted a portion of the town's southern border for the new highway cut through the limestone hills.

As the massive earthmovers scraped away tons of earth and rock, numerous previously unknown cave openings were exposed in the brittle limestone. These gaping entrances beckoned inquisitive, willing boys into subterranean mystery amid the dusty, noisy and bone-rattling road construction mayhem.

Here, on May 10, 1967, the largest cave search in US history began to unfold, involving hundreds of volunteers and many of the nation's best caving experts.

The cavers joined local, county and state emergency responders to search above and below ground for the missing trio. It was a race against time. Nerves would fray, and partisan bickering developed among the cavers who disliked what they considered grandstanding by William Karras, president of the newly formed Speleological Society of America (SSA), a new Washington, DC-based cave search and rescue organization. Karras brought to Hannibal his desire for raising awareness of cave rescue, a flare for public relations, and a controversial past.

Still, the cavers and other rescue personnel worked heroically and tirelessly day and night, faithfully doing their jobs. They left nothing unchecked. Caves large and small, forested hollows, barns, garages, sheds, wells, the nearby river and its islands, all were carefully searched, then searched again.

This epic human endeavor would provide another compelling chapter in Hannibal's history. The search would soon make American caving history, marking the first time cave search and rescue personnel would fail to find the lost explorers they were seeking.

***

This book, the most comprehensive assessment of the event, details the story of America's largest cave calamity and search operation. Its intent is to historically preserve the memories of Joel, Billy and Craig so they are not forgotten victims in a heroic story that's remained largely untold until now. *Lost Boys* is my attempt to recognize the brave and heroic efforts by Hannibal and Quincy (IL) area residents and others who left their own hometowns throughout the states of Missouri, Illinois, and beyond, to come and help search for the boys.

As a thirteen-year-old boy who spent his childhood in Hannibal and nearby Quincy, I was an eyewitness to the massive search that was launched after the boys' shocking disappearance. In a seeming instant, a friend and fellow childhood adventurer Joel Hoag, his younger brother Billy, and their friend Craig Dowell simply vanished. I recall standing along Birch Street with my father, Bud, and my younger brother, Brad, watching with the gathered throng of onlookers as the search teams worked feverishly around the clock.

Joel was a classmate of mine during the elementary school years at the original A.D. Stowell School, located across the street from the Hoag family home on Fulton Avenue, just a block or so southwest of the Highway 79 roadcut. Joel loved to explore, and at night he gazed at the stars through his telescope and dreamed of being an astronaut.

Younger brother Billy was an active, curious kid with freckles and a mop of reddish hair who was always tagging along with the older boys.

Edwin, who was called Craig, had an open friendly face, usually sporting a smile. He lived on Union Street, right behind the Hoag's house on Fulton Avenue. Craig was serious and polite, but usually a willing accomplice for many of the neighborhood adventures.

I came to learn much more about the Hoags and Dowells in discussions with relatives and friends who still to this day desperately miss them and wonder what happened.

As an adult in middle age, I've been drawn to write about this Hannibal mystery. The historic story, and the boys, must not be forgotten. The responders and volunteers, the heroes of this story, must be honored, too. Those distant memories of childhood evolved into a longing curiosity to know more about what transpired. Were lingering questions still unanswerable or had new clues about the lost boys surfaced since 1967?

On a blustery day some years ago, I stood atop Lover's Leap, the three-hundred-foot-high bluff overlook which serves as the town's most prominent geologic feature. The view is spectacular up and down the Mississippi river. On a clear day, the tallest buildings are visible in downtown Quincy, Illinois, seventeen miles upstream. To the east, the view is of rich Illinois river bottom land that produces robust corn and soybean yields. Outstretched below is the hilly town of Hannibal, looking like a picture postcard.

I recall a day, more than five decades earlier, when I was playing on this very spot with Joel Hoag and lifelong friend Gary Rush. Scrambling down along the face of the Lover's Leap overlook, we followed a narrow dirt path until we climbed up into a sheltered area beneath the Leap's rocky point.

It was dangerous scrambling, but for three curious boys the rocky feature offered a perfect hideout. Amid the loose, brittle rock, we drank in the spectacular views of the Mississippi river, the pastoral town, and the verdant farmland beyond. Many idyllic summer afternoons were spent here during childhood, as we told stories and shot our BB guns and slingshots at imagined foes on the river.

That was the last time I saw Joel Hoag.

What brought me to Lover's Leap on this windy spring day was neither the view nor the memories of those idle hours of youth. It was the simple, small granite marker placed there in memory of three lost boys whose adventures ended too soon. It is a gravestone, too—perhaps.

Even today, no one can be *absolutely* certain what happened to Joel Hoag, Billy Hoag, and Edwin Craig Dowell during the late afternoon of May 10, 1967. As the boys' mothers called them for dinner, and siblings set out in search of their brothers, there was no sign of them. No boys with tousled hair and dusty sneakers came running home. They had simply vanished.

People still speculate about their fate. Cavers who participated in the massive search to this day ponder the mystery during reflective moments. They find themselves wondering whether they missed important clues. Should they have searched longer, looked elsewhere, dug further into those seemingly endless cave passages? Did police aggressively investigate the possibility of foul play? Was there any possibility the boys ran away? Or, were they accidentally buried alive by the heavy construction equipment that had exposed the vast maze cave complex below the roadbed, an irresistible draw for the curious boys in the days and hours leading up to their disappearance.

Many people still grieve for the boys and their families, shaking their heads in frustration, some shedding tears as they share recollections. Family members have gone to their graves not knowing what happened to their sons and brothers. Many of the boys' siblings and friends live quiet lives not far from where the boys roamed and were last seen. They all still wonder.

The search took on a carnival-like atmosphere at times, with onlookers offering their own theories about what happened. Even psychics were called to Hannibal to attempt to identify the boys' whereabouts. Their impressions offer provocative fodder for those who still speculate about the boys' shared fate. Others had their own frightening theory, one involving murder and cover-up.

The search for the lost boys of Hannibal is a compelling, heart-wrenching story wrapped in adventure and mystery, all taking place in a town known and beloved worldwide as the boyhood home of humorist Samuel Clemens and the literary setting for so many of the stories he wrote under his pen name, Mark Twain.

On May 10, 1967, in a nation wracked by anti-war protests and cultural turmoil, this historic community lost part of its innocence and emerged into the national headlines for a very different reason. Still, the final chapter of this mystery remains unwritten. After a half century, the fate of Joel, Billy, and Craig remains the ultimate unsolved mystery.

John Wingate
Minneapolis, Minnesota
December 2017

Chapter 1

The Last Day

One day you're up
When you turn around
You find your world is tumbling down
It happened to me...

Lyrics from *The Happening* by The Supremes
#1 song in the US May 10, 1967

It's always midnight in a cave; the perpetual, inky darkness is all-enveloping. Not a photon of light is available for human eyes in this subterranean world. *Total* darkness. You can't tell whether your eyes are open or closed. A hand waved in front of your face goes unseen.

Caves are cool and damp, often coffin-snug, with a gaping abyss possibly lurking ahead for the explorer. A simple stumble and fall of a few feet in this rocky environment can be debilitating, even fatal. Lying on the cold cave floor will sap your body heat in hours, bringing on hypothermia. So a caver's every action, every footstep, every move requires not only the light from a dependable headlamp, but careful training and reliable equipment. Lighting drives the whole experience because you cannot expect to find your way out of most caves in total darkness. Without illumination, inexperienced cave explorers will quickly succumb to primal fears as the suffocating darkness and chill close around them.

Fear of the dark is called nyctophobia, from the Greek word for night—nyx. Many people have some fear of darkness, which can magnify anxieties and worries. The subterranean environment can prey upon the mind of even the most experienced caver. Claustrophobia and anxiety may become psychological companions in the dark underground. Temporal distortions impact your perception of time and your sleep patterns. Insomnia and auditory and visual hallucinations can develop if a caver stays underground long enough.

The informed caver will tell you their sport is not for the inexperienced and faint of heart. When you enter a cave, considerable technical skills are demanded, and sound judgment is paramount. In other words, caving favors the prepared.

But on this spring day, three risk-taking Hannibal boys with no caving expertise, but an abundance of bravado, made Hannibal ground zero for a terrifying, unfolding calamity that would leave its traumatic mark on the river town for half a century.

* * *

Worst fears became real as the May 11, 1967 *Quincy Herald-Whig* newspaper headline jumped from the top of the front page:

3 Boys Still Missing in Cave

I read on, not fully comprehending the extraordinary nature of the story, shocked to discover these Hannibal boys, ages eleven to fourteen, one of them a good friend from my five years attending Hannibal's Stowell Elementary School, were believed to be missing in the sprawling and complex Murphy's Cave on the Missouri town's sedate Southside.

My friend Joel Hoag, his younger brother Billy, and their friend Edwin Craig Dowell were last seen the previous afternoon near several cave entrances that were exposed during highway construction work.

"This is terrible!" I exclaimed to my parents as we hovered over the paper.

We'd moved to Quincy, Illinois, seventeen miles up the Mississippi River from Hannibal, in June 1964, after I had completed fifth grade at A.D. Stowell School, but I well remembered Joel and his insatiable interest in exploration and natural history. And Billy was always tagging along with the older boys. *How could this happen*, I pondered, as my thirteen-year-old brain struggled to absorb the tragic news.

After supper, we watched the six o'clock news on WGEM-TV and learned that dozens of cavers from throughout the region and as far away as Washington, DC were beginning to arrive in Hannibal.

Later, I struggled to focus as I tackled homework, the tragedy intruding on my concentration. I finally closed the books and settled on the sofa to watch *My Three Sons* on KHQA. Three sons—three boys—I couldn't catch a break. I struggled to rein in the emotion welling up as my throat tightened. At age thirteen, a boy never fully reveals his feelings. It was an immutable rule seemingly burned into our boyish DNA.

Finally, at ten p.m. I was off to bed. Lying in the darkness of my second story bedroom, the tears finally came, my eyes brimming over, as reality hit home. "Where could they be?" I asked God. "Please let the boys be found."

Three lost boys, barely halfway to manhood, were facing an uncertain fate. At our ages, life lay ahead ready to unfold full of promise and opportunity. But what would the future hold for my gregarious buddy Joel and the other two boys? Would they ever know the joy of true love, the beauty of their child's birth? Would Joel ever fulfill his longing to become a scientist? Would Billy and Craig reach their life potential?

Kids weren't accustomed to losing their friends. We'd said goodbye and buried grandparents, aunts and uncles, but never childhood friends. Life was just beginning. It was all still new.

While it was too early to think the worst, everyone fell into a dark, worrisome mood as we anxiously waited for fate to reveal its hand.

* * *

The previous day, May 10, 1967, dawned overcast and cool in Northeast Missouri. The countryside's emerging shades of green were a gift to the eyes. The few scattered sun rays peeking through the cloud layer made the dewy leaves and grass appear sprinkled with gleaming diamonds. The early morning humidity hung like an etheric wisp over the Marion County countryside.

May is typically the wettest month, as gardeners, cavers and other outdoor enthusiasts know. Three inches of rain had already fallen. By afternoon, the high temperature would hit seventy-seven degrees, a nice day during this cool, wet spring.

Many residents were busily preparing their garden plots and planting vegetables and flowers. Mushroom hunters were grabbing their grocery sacks and exploring the wooded hills and valleys of Marion County in search of the prized morels.

Out on the Mississippi river, a tug pushing a brood of barges bellowed a mournful wail as she chugged slowly downstream, bringing coal for factories and power plants from St. Louis to New Orleans.

At Standard Printing Company, the town's century-old business, the clanking printing presses were being greased and inked for another day's run.

School children were anxiously awaiting the start of summer vacation in a few weeks. And tourists were coming to town, spending their dollars and enjoying the Mark Twain-themed venues and shops. *America's Hometown* was on the cusp of another robust summer of play and tourism.

On Third Street, reporter Herb Powell sauntered into the Becky Thatcher Café for coffee, before heading to work at the *Hannibal Courier-Post* newspaper across the street. Herb liked the morning routine at the popular restaurant. He'd take the pulse of the community, pick up some good news tips and mix with local business and community leaders. Amid the clatter of dishes and caffeine-fueled conversations, breakfast patrons perused their newspapers, the stories revealing a nation in turmoil.

Across the US, antiwar protests were building to a fever pitch as the Vietnam War raged half a world away. America was fast approaching the *Summer of Love* in San Francisco which would define the decade with psychedelic rock, growing drug use, and an emerging hippie movement, its mantra sung by the Beatles, The Doors, The Rolling Stones, and Jimi Hendrix. As hair grew longer, trust in the establishment diminished. Dissent became the norm on many college campuses. Americans were horrified by news coming from Chicago where Richard Speck was on trial for the murders of eight student nurses.

Elvis Presley, the "King of Rock and Roll," and his new bride Priscilla were enjoying their honeymoon. A man given the moniker *Mister Rogers* prepared for the May 22 premiere of his new children's program on national public television. And Americans marveled at the first heart transplants performed by South African surgeon Christiaan Barnard, MD.

Before the summer of '67 ended, Americans would be shocked by the race riots that rocked Detroit and more than one hundred other US cities, and the horrific, fatal grizzly attacks on two female campers in popular Glacier National Park. For Americans, 1967 would prove to be a year of big, tragic stories, as Hannibalians would soon discover in a profoundly personal way.

State Highway 79 construction site, May 1967. Photo by Jerry Vineyard

As pastoral Hannibal stirred this morning, highway construction workers resumed their labors on the town's southern border. The workers were improving Highway 79 to more directly connect Hannibal with the nearby towns of Ilasco, Louisiana—another former riverboat boomtown—and onward to its southern terminus in suburban St. Louis. This portion of the *Great River Road* through the high Lincoln Hills bluffs would offer a spectacular view of the nearby Mississippi and the rolling countryside (Highway 79 was designated part of the *National Scenic Byways Program* in 1991).

Route 79 was first built in the 1930s, but by the 1960s the narrow road was long overdue for improvement. Commercial planners wanted to develop the area south of Hannibal and a wide, modern highway was essential. An improved State Highway 79 would be an ever-important artery to showcase the scenic beauty of Mississippi river country and keep communities connected for the substantial economic benefits that flow from tourism and other commercial activities from Northeast Missouri to the St. Louis metropolitan area.

In 1967, if you hopped in your car near the downtown Mark Twain Museum and drove south on Main Street for several blocks, you would cross Bear Creek, a sluggish muddy ribbon of water defining the northern geographic border for Hannibal's Southside. The collection of neat, older homes beyond were occupied by middle class families solid in faith and work ethic.

By necessity, their little community within a community—the Southside—had its own elementary school, fire department, many small grocery stores, and a few drug stores and churches. Passing trains often blocked the Southside from the rest of town for long, inconvenient periods. This would soon change as an overhead viaduct spanning Bear Creek and the rail line was part of the Highway 79 project. Progress was on the march.

Just before eight o'clock in the morning, a screen door slammed with a loud crack, shattering the morning quiet along a stretch of Fulton Avenue. Joel Hoag dashed across the front porch of his family's rambling, two-story whitewashed home on his way to catch the school bus. The good-natured thirteen-year-old, juggling books and a sack lunch, ticked off one more day on his mental calendar. The end of the school year was only a few weeks away. *I'll be free,* he surely thought. Joel, an inquisitive teen in a robust family of eleven children, loved science, especially astronomy and natural history.

Joel's younger brother Billy, eleven, was a freckled, blue-eyed redhead who loved to tease and joke around. He was usually found with the older kids looking for fun. Billy attended fifth grade at Stowell School across the street from the Hoag home.

Their friend Edwin Craig Dowell, fourteen, who lived at 600 Union Street, right behind the Hoag home, was an easy-going teen who liked pullover sweaters and wingtip shoes, popular teen garb in that era. Craig enjoyed tinkering with bicycles and was a polite, curious and inquisitive young man, according to friends. "Craig was a nice guy, kind of quiet. We played a lot of basketball together on the playground. I always felt he was kind of a loner," a childhood friend recalled.

The Hoag boys and their playmates loved the outdoors and were already making plans for another summer of exploration among the Southside's forested hills and bluffs. Hannibal's lush countryside was a second home for them when the weather cooperated. The boys found real adventures, like those Joel had read about in his dog-eared copy of Mark Twain's *The Adventures of Tom Sawyer.*

From the valleys and rocky bluffs in the nearby hills, the boys brought home snakes and other critters to show their friends. I recall one particular school day in fourth grade when Joel brought a thick, six-foot-long black snake across the street to show the kids after school. The girls screamed, recoiling in horror at the sight of the monstrous reptile, but the boys jostled each other and moved closer for a better look. Joel had draped the serpent over his shoulders, his hands extended outward, holding the head and tail.

"I found it on my uncle's farm," he told us. "It looks like he's had plenty of mice to eat," Joel exclaimed, ever the young naturalist proud of his find.

Hannibal kids spent most of their days outdoors back then, before the Internet, portable devices and hundreds of cable channels posed distractions. Along eroded drainages in the nearby hills, Indian arrowheads that had washed from their centuries-old resting places lay in wait for observant, young eyes to discover them. Walking creekbeds and searching cliff faces, the boys found fossil-encrusted chunks of brittle Burlington Limestone. They explored the numerous small cave openings throughout the countryside of hilly Hannibal. It was all so captivating, and it left the youngsters dreaming for more as darkness capped those long, carefree days of childhood.

Joel and the other boys were especially excited about the massive Highway 79 road construction project just a few blocks from their homes. It was a natural boy-magnet. Construction crews manning huge earthmovers and steam shovels were doing dangerous work. Loud booms had been heard for many days as the road crew dynamited limestone and earth. They moved millions of tons of dirt and stone as they transformed the once-forested hills into a modern scenic highway—Hannibal's gateway to and from points south.

Joel, Billy, and Craig had made an exciting discovery earlier in the week as they watched the road construction activity from their high perch on the rocky roadcut through which the highway roadbed extended. As the earthmover's blades scraped and leveled the surface of the roadbed, several limestone cave openings were exposed, entry points into a previously unknown labyrinth of complex subterranean passages beneath this area of the Southside.

"Look at that!" Joel likely exclaimed, pointing down to one of the roadbed openings. The boys all agreed these newly-opened cave passages had to be explored. They quickly departed for the Hoag house where they fashioned a crude ladder to ease their entry into the beckoning cave openings and returned ready to go.

As the boys descended through the dust cloud into one of the cave openings, their eyes were likely as big as saucers. They were getting their first look at this amazing new world, as the rumble of the large earthmovers overhead now sounded muffled and distant. Joel swung the flashlight around and found the cave passages dry, spreading out in many directions like tentacles. In spots, the cave's ceiling was at least twice their height, and the passages, generally narrower at the top and bottom, were up to six feet across at the widest spot.

"This is amazing," one of the boys exclaimed as the trio absorbed the grandeur of that incredible boy-cave.

They thought this new find was as amazing as nearby Mark Twain Cave, a nationally known show cave, and Cameron Cave, a wild cave left in its natural state across Cave Hollow from its companion show cave. Both caves lie just a mile south of the boys' roadcut location. These Hannibal area caves are complex maze caves, sculpted eons ago by the waters of an ancient sea that receded, leaving the Mississippi River and the cave networks in place. The caves contain impossibly complex labyrinths of criss-crossed passages lined with rough limestone ledges that can tear skin and clothing. Many of the nation's most complex and spectacular maze caves are located in northeast Missouri.

The boys proceeded slowly, often coming to other passages that were barely large enough to squeeze through. In some spots, they dropped to their hands and feet to make it through low passages half full of ancient silt. As the boys crawled along, dust and small bits of rock rained down on them from the ceiling as the mechanized vibrations from above shook the earth. What they likely did not notice were the thousands of accumulating hairline fractures in the limestone strata, the product of many days of dynamite blasting and earthmoving.

This first visit was cut short because the boys had to get home, but they talked about exploring more of the cave system in the days ahead. As they climbed out of the cave onto the dusty, noisy roadbed, the boys' joyful reverie was interrupted by a highway worker yelling at them to leave the work zone.

"This is a dangerous place for you kids," the man sternly warned. The boys were told the heavy earthmoving equipment was constantly moving, shaking the ground and kicking up dust, reducing visibility. "Go on home! You could get hurt!"

Still, the exuberant boys' lust for adventure persisted. On Tuesday, May 9, they returned, again darting across the roadbed and entering another gaping cave opening. After exploring for a while, they emerged from their subterranean hangout and headed home, their clothes and shoes caked with mud from the roadbed left messy by recent rain.

The Hoag parents, Mike and Helen, were furious when Billy and Joel showed up looking like ragamuffins with nervous grins on their dirty faces.

A Hoag sibling, sixteen-year-old Debbie, heard the tongue-lashing the boys received from their parents. "They said if you go in those (cave openings) again you're going to get your motor oiled, and that meant they were going to get a paddling. So, the boys had to go and wash their clothes and clean their shoes," Debbie later told a reporter.

***

At Hannibal Junior High School, on the city's northwest edge, the school day on May 10 crawled along, as they usually do near the end of the academic year. When the final bell signaled the end of studies, Joel double-timed it to his locker and stowed his books before the fifteen-minute bus ride home. Always the inquisitive teen, and likely conflicted by his parents' warnings to avoid the caves, Joel had mentally made plans to do *something* outdoors on this fine spring day.

Craig Dowell came running down the hallway, skidding to a stop on the polished marble floor, nearly running into fellow Southsider Steve Sederwall. "Steve, be sure to save me a seat on the church bus," Sederwall remembers Craig saying. Both teens, who often worshipped at Southside Christian Church, were planning to attend the Wednesday night youth gathering that rotated among the area's Christian churches. "I can still clearly picture Craig in my mind," Sederwall recalled decades later. "He had on black cuffed pants, a gray and black pullover sweater and wingtips. He always wore wingtips." Sederwall, who would spend more than forty years as a police officer and cold case investigator, had excellent observation skills even at age sixteen. "I was one of the last people to see Craig at school," he stated. "I remember the moment clearly."

Back at the Hoag house, Helen Hoag looked out the door and shouted to son Tim, fifteen, as he stepped off the high school bus, instructing him to watch Joel and Billy so they would not go exploring the caves again. "Keep an eye on the boys, and don't let them leave the yard," Debbie remembers her saying. The Hoag parents departed for the grocery store, satisfied they'd put an end to this cave exploring nonsense.

After school, Joel changed into jeans and a white T-shirt and headed out the front door, again reminded by Debbie to stay in the yard. Shortly, he caught up with Billy and Craig to hang out and play, the three mindful of the warnings to stay away from the caves.

What they could not know was that they had just been to their last day of school—forever—and fate was writing a new final chapter of their lives.

***

The boys were so excited about their recent cave discoveries they were more than willing to try to recruit their friends to join the next adventure.

Rob Yager, who was the same age as Billy Hoag, had more interest in mini-bikes and go-carts than caving. "Billy was an adventurous boy, nice and always smiling. I enjoyed being with him," Yager said. "I liked cycling in the woods, but we often were out together rock climbing, looking for snakes, kid stuff."

On May 10, Billy had approached Yager in the hallway of Stowell School with an invitation. "He came up and invited me to explore the caves after school. He said they were going to explore a new one they had found. I refused because my Dad wouldn't allow it," Yager explained. "As Dad put it, 'No way in Hell.'"

Deborah Roberson-White, now a Nashville, Tennessee resident, was seventeen in 1967 and lived across the street from the Stowell School playground, just a few doors away from the school itself. On May 10, she exited the school bus near Burns' Grocery at Fulton and Riverside Street, a short distance from the roadcut. She walked home to change clothes and then headed back to meet her friend Sue Mudd who lived next door to the Southside Christian Church parsonage. "In front of Stowell, Joel and Billy stopped me and said they were going into the caves, and invited Sue and I to go," Robeson-White explained. "I told them, 'No thanks boys, and you shouldn't go in them either.' I was always protective of the neighborhood kids, but they went on their way and were heading to Murphy's Cave." The time was shortly after four p.m.

***

John Janes, whose family had moved to the Southside in 1966, attended eighth grade with Joel and Craig at Hannibal Junior High School. Although new to town, John had already explored parts of another subterranean cave network known as Murphy's Cave, located just three blocks north of the Highway 79 roadcut construction zone.

"Near Walnut and Birch Streets, there was a Murphy's Cave opening that had long been sealed, but it was exposed again during the road construction," Janes explained. "It was pretty routine for kids to go in there. We all thought we were spelunkers. What teenage boy wouldn't... it was *there*," he added, reflecting on his adolescent mindset for adventure.

On the bus ride home from school, Janes and his friend Lynn Strube discussed the cave and decided to explore it again. "We got home, changed clothes and rode our bikes down to Murphy's. We'd gone into the cave two or three times with flashlights in the past, but not very far, just far enough we were confident we could find our way back out," Janes said.

By Janes estimation, he and Lynn had entered the cave about four p.m. on May 10. "The passages were very small, branching this way and that, and we had to crawl on our belly to get through some of them. We could sit up in some areas, but none of the areas in this particular part of the cave were high enough to stand," Janes said.

Meanwhile, outside the cave, Wes Leffert came rolling down Walnut Street shortly past four p.m. on his beloved green Huffy bike tricked out with banana seat and high-rise handlebars. The saddlebag baskets over the rear wheel were packed with *Quincy Herald-Whig* newspapers he delivered seven days a week to Southside homes.

As Leffert approached Birch street he noticed Joel, Billy and Craig standing by the Murphy's Cave entrance. "As I rode up they stopped me. They were getting ready to go in and wanted to know if I wanted to go with them. I told them I had to deliver papers, and to be careful. It was good they had a flashlight because, once you're inside, the passages went in many directions, and it's pitch black in the cave."

After exploring Murphy's Cave for about twenty minutes, Janes and Strube had turned around and reversed their course out of the cave. "As we were coming out of the muddy entrance, we met Craig, Joel and Billy standing outside waiting to come in. They weren't muddy so we knew they hadn't been inside yet. I think they had flashlights with them, because you didn't get into that cave very far before you lost daylight."

Janes and Strube stopped and chatted with the boys for a few minutes before mounting their bikes and rolling down the sidewalk. "As we left, I looked back and saw them going into the cave. That was the last time we saw them, probably about 4:30," Janes said.

Half an hour later, about five p.m., motorist Wayne Woodson drove past Southside Christian Church, situated next to the roadcut construction area. He noticed a young boy who fit the description of Billy walking near the roadcut carrying a small military-type shovel. He thought it curious given the heavy activity at the road construction site. What would the boy be doing with that shovel?

One of the last individuals to see the boys was retired school teacher Louise Kohler, now in her late nineties. She spent most of her career as a dedicated second grade teacher at A.D. Stowell School. Kohler lived near the Hoags and literally across Fulton Avenue from the school, giving her a daily commute measured in seconds. She got along well with the neighborhood kids. "Those boys were nice, no trouble with them," she recalled. "I liked them, they were always polite and seemed intelligent. They were only being boys going out and exploring," Kohler added, revealing a teacher's understanding of the nature of teenage boys.

Kohler had first seen the boys after school as they meandered down the alley behind her house, talking and kicking rocks with their rubber-toed sneakers. She briefly spoke with the boys who told her they were going to the Stowell playground down the block, appearing to obey their parents' directive to avoid the roadcut caves.

Kohler departed shortly for a teacher's meeting across town, but ended up leaving the gathering early because she wasn't feeling well. "On my way back home, this was shortly after five p.m., I saw the boys standing high up on the sloping roadcut, looking down at the big earthmovers. I knew it was them because I recognized their clothing from when I'd seen them earlier that afternoon." Kohler saw the boys at the roadcut location three blocks south of the Walnut and Birch location where Leffert, Janes and Strube had seen the trio less than an hour earlier. The boys, tempted by adventure, had returned to the very spot the Hoag parents had warned them to avoid.

Meanwhile, janitor Thomas Breedlove was finishing up his custodial duties on the second floor of Stowell School. While emptying wastebaskets, he'd glanced out a window about 4:40 p.m. and saw the three boys cutting across a lawn heading toward the roadcut. Half an hour later, he wrapped up his duties by closing and locking the windows in room 202. He again looked out over the rooftops and saw the boys standing on the high slope on the east side of the roadcut where Mrs. Kohler had seen them minutes earlier. He watched them for a moment and then moved along. The time was 5:15 p.m.

Even at that hour, the roadcut site was a chaotic scene. Large earthmovers were lumbering back and forth, the ground vibrating, the air filling with swirling, choking dust causing poor visibility in the immediate area. When the dust cloud briefly dissipated, the boys had vanished from the hillside.

Given the circumstances, three boys dashing into this dusty maelstrom could easily be missed by the busy workers. After all, they'd done so earlier in the week when the trio had entered gaping holes in the roadbed and disappeared into the cave system below, discovered only when they later emerged.

The busy workmen would continue to grade the dusty roadbed, oblivious to the boys' underground presence, perhaps even filling in a cave opening and sealing the boys' fate.

What we know with certainty is that after 5:15 p.m. on May 10, 1967, Joel Hoag, Billy Hoag, and Craig Dowell were never seen again.

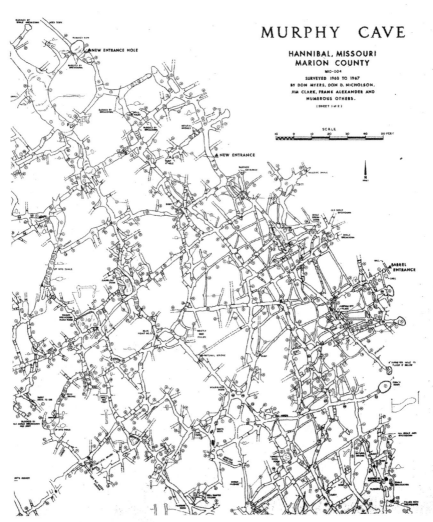

A portion of the Murphy's Cave map.
Courtesy Missouri Speleological Survey.

Chapter 2

Calamity at Nightfall

About 5:15 p.m., David Bentley, fourteen, a friend of Joel and Billy Hoag, stopped at the Hoag house to see the boys. Mrs. Hoag answered the door smiling and told him the boys were out playing. "If you see them tell them to hurry home if they want to go to the church youth meeting with Craig," Mrs. Hoag told Bentley, according to the Speleological Society of America's after-action report.

Meanwhile, older brother Tim Hoag left the house about 5:45 p.m. to look for the boys. He spoke with neighborhood kids who had seen the trio enter Murphy's Cave at Walnut and Birch streets. Tim, convinced the boys were still in the cave, headed back home to get a flashlight when the passing church bus loaded with teens caught his eye. "Hey Tim! Tim Hoag!" yelled a friend, waving from the window of the passing church bus.

Steve Sederwall, who was aboard the bus, had noticed that neither Craig Dowell nor the Hoag boys had showed up to attend the church rally. "Craig's older brother, Mike, was angry Craig wasn't joining us. He said, 'He can just miss the meeting!'" Sederwall recalled.

Soon, Helen and Mike Hoag joined Tim at the Murphy's Cave entrance. Helen shouted for the boys, and after getting no response decided more search help was needed. Gripped with concern, she hurried to the nearby home of a friend and called Hannibal police at 6:26 p.m. Officers arrived in a few minutes and entered the cave, proceeding as if they were entering an alien world, decked out in their uniforms and shiny leather shoes. "Craaaig! Joelll! Billlly! Are you in here?" No answer.

***

The Hoag family was well known in town, given their eleven active and friendly children, whose ages spanned more than two decades. When the Hoags, who didn't own a car, had a family portrait taken, it took two cabs to take the family downtown to Herring Studios. "Mom knew the kids would be messy if they walked downtown so we cabbed it," said Dorothea Lynn (Lynnie) Hoag-Pedigo, the third oldest child.

Helen's and Mike's family-friendly eatery and watering hole, Hoag's Tavern, was a popular venue known for its delicious tamales, meatloaf sandwiches and homemade pies. The parents worked hard, and the kids were often on their own for hours at a time. "We took care of each other. It was fun having so many kids in the house," said Lynnie. "I can remember when Dan, Robin, and Denise were all in diapers and I'd rock all three at the same time. As the older kids grew up, we got to help be Santa Claus and the Easter Bunny. It was fun."

At home, the children loved the regular Friday night ritual. Mike Hoag would bring home a five-gallon container of vanilla ice cream and make malts and french toast for the large brood. "It was a smart, fun way to fill us up," Lynnie said. Lynnie especially remembers sitting on her dad's lap sharing a cinnamon roll dunked in coffee. "We were all Daddy's girls and boys." In the summer, Mike would often grill hamburgers for all the kids in the neighborhood.

News of the missing boys quickly began to spread, and people turned out to join the well-liked Hoag parents and siblings in a foot search of the neighborhoods.

John Lyng, then twenty, was attending Hannibal LaGrange College and interning at the *Courier-Post* newspaper as a cub reporter and photographer. On May 10, he was covering the annual

Marion County Civil Defense preparedness drill at the Naval Reserve building. Police officers, firefighters and several members of the Mark Twain Emergency Squad were on the scene as participants.

"Suddenly, a call came in that there was a *real* search to undertake," Lyng said. Bill Bridges, the vice-commander of the emergency squad, ordered the volunteer members called out. The Mark Twain Emergency Squad had been created in 1962, and while the volunteers had extensive experience pulling bodies out of the Mississippi, responding to vehicle accidents, and finding lost hunters in the woods, they had no experience with a cave search or rescue situation.

Bridges called Northeast Power's Superintendent Mike Boudreau and asked him to send heavy equipment, drilling gear and jack hammers to the Murphy's Cave site. "Soon it looked like a parade coming down the street with all that equipment lined up heading to the Southside," Lyng said.

Mark Twain Emergency Squad volunteers, led by Bridges and squad Commander Bob Harrison, arrived to aid in the search at 7:55 p.m., an understandable delay since squad volunteers held regular jobs and had to gather their personal gear before responding to a call.

Squad member Willard 'Woody' St. Clair, who worked for the Hannibal Board of Public Works, had been across town atop a power pole replacing a transformer when his radio crackled to life with the urgent call for assistance on the Southside. "There were about twenty of us in the squad at that time. We all showed up in our coveralls and brought the rescue gear we thought we'd need— shovels, picks, lights and a backhoe, but we didn't have any caving equipment at the time," St. Clair said.

According to St. Clair, the squad members split up, some going to Murphy's Cave while others went to the roadcut area to the south. St. Clair quickly established a roped security perimeter around the construction site, and emergency squad members cautiously entered a gaping hole in the roadbed that had been graded recently by the heavy equipment. "We were told the roadbed was like a fragile shell. We'd driven one of our big trucks onto it to unload equipment, but having seen the cave holes they told us to hurry, worried the roadway might collapse. Still, we had to move the truck real slowly to minimize any vibration."

A gathering crowd continued to build through the evening as St. Clair kept the onlookers a safe distance from the roadbed. "People were always trying to get closer and lean in to see better. The hardest part was keeping the family members at a distance. It was painful for them, difficult to keep them away." It had rained earlier in the day, so the emergency squad team quietly wondered if the moisture had possibly weakened the soil, contributing to a cave collapse that trapped the boys somewhere.

Rescue personnel work feverishly overnight to widen a roadcut opening into the cave system below. Photo courtesy Hannibal Courier-Post.

The Emergency Squad team members, none with any caving expertise, explored the roadbed cave into the early morning hours and were forced to dig out some areas of collapsed debris in the cave passages. "They said it appeared the contractor had already dumped some dirt and rocky debris into another hole, so they tried to dig around the blockage to see if the boys were in there, but they found no evidence of them." Another team was dispatched to explore a cave discovered near the Saverton Lock and Dam south of the roadcut several miles, but nothing was found.

Concurrently, other squad members cautiously entered Murphy's Cave, carefully exploring the immediate passages and calling out the boys' names. As they moved through the small passageways, they marked the cold limestone walls with chalk and unfurled string so they could find their way out later. The men would explore one passage only to come upon several others branching off, and each of those passages would eventually branch off into others. "It was just left-right-left right," said one rescue worker. It was visually chaotic, and the squad members had no idea how far the cave system continued as they worried about themselves becoming lost. "There were many passages that just ended, so you didn't know if it was a recent collapse or had always been that way. You'd have to open all of them up to be completely thorough, perhaps an impossible feat given the confines of the vast cave," said St. Clair.

Murphy's Cave is yet another maze cave in Northeast Missouri, they learned. Most passages must be explored crawling on all fours or walking hunched over for hours on end due to the low ceilings. It was grueling search work. Each passage largely appeared the same as the others, tan in color with packed clay floors. Soon, the rescue squad volunteers were meeting each other as they wound their way through the cave's tangle of passages.

"It's certainly a vast cave system," St. Clair surmised. "A local caver, Carl Jacobson, told me he'd explored much of the area cave system and believed some of the passages stretched for miles." Jacobson is now deceased.

31

By now, more townspeople were gathering outside of Murphy's Cave. Word had spread, and everyone assumed their roles in the drama as curious bystanders seeking any nugget of information about the boys' whereabouts. "I was now handling security at the scene," St. Clair added. "We had to keep onlookers and family members in safe areas. We didn't need anyone else getting lost or hurt."

Craig Dowell's mother, Helen, a cook at the Becky Thatcher restaurant, was on the scene feeling anxious and frustrated, dabbing her eyes with a Kleenex. "We've talked to him, talked to him, talked to him, about going into these caves," she told *Courier-Post* reporter Herb Powell, the frustration evident in her voice. "But he's still a boy."

This was Powell's kind of story; he was a good reporter and got along well with people. "Herb was very trustworthy and had good sources around town," said *Courier-Post* editor Howard Hoffmaster who led the eight-person newsroom in 1967.

"Powell had gotten a tip about the missing boys from a police source and called me, so I joined him at the scene about 8:30 that night," Hoffmaster said. Both newsmen did double-duty initially, helping to search for the boys while gathering the facts for tomorrow's top-of-the-front-page story. "We went into the caves and looked for traces of the boys, any footprints, equipment or evidence of collapses. What we found were lots of footprints from the searchers." The two newsmen went their separate ways inside the cave. Herb Powell moved more slowly because of a shortened, crippled leg, the consequence of a childhood accident.

"I was trying to imagine what had happened to the boys, so I was very cautious," Hoffmaster explained. "When I got to a point where I felt unsure, I'd carefully back out. We were in there three or four hours doing a series of short probes of many passages. It didn't take long for us to realize we were in a real labyrinth."

Hoffmaster, who was born in St. Paul and raised in Winona, Minnesota, both Mississippi river towns like Hannibal, stayed with the search until about midnight, hopeful the boys had just wandered off and would soon return. He quickly compared notes with Herb who had busily been interviewing police and sheriff's department sources, then returned to the downtown newsroom to begin writing the story for the *Courier-Post's* May 11 afternoon edition.

As Hoffmaster arrived at the newspaper offices, the intensity and urgency of the search captured his mind like few stories ever would. "The cavers all commented on how hard it was to search the confusing cave, how much rubble there was inside. Many were still clinging to the bias that the boys were out somewhere on a lark."

In the coming days, news developments would unfold quickly as Powell spent 90 percent of his time on the search story, and Hoffmaster split his time between the big story and his other editorial duties at the newspaper. "I don't recall sleeping at all initially. My wife didn't see me those first two days," Hoffmaster said.

Cub reporter John Lyng meanwhile had been working the story all evening. He'd discovered that grocer Cornelius Murphy had long ago operated a small grocery store at Walnut and Birch and used the ancient cave for cold storage. The cave had been closed for many years, until road construction exposed a hillside opening into the cave system. Highway workers told Lyng the widening of Birch Street just north of Walnut had attracted lots of kids who'd gone into the cave in recent days, worrisome news for anxious Southside parents who were just now learning of the danger.

Lyng reflected on his own Hannibal childhood as he worked the story. As a child, he had lived at Fourth and Hill Streets and often played in the Cardiff Hill area near the Hannibal Lighthouse. "There were lots of cliffs, ledges, deep woods, and plenty of danger for us." He realized his own boyhood was a haunting foreshadowing of this growing, breaking story.

Milton Martin, a Kroger store employee who had just turned twenty, was driving home to the Southside about nine p.m. when he noticed the search activity, the darkness being cut by search lights set up by the rescue squad. Milton had been in Murphy's Cave many times during his youth, thanks to a hidden entrance that most everyone of his generation knew about. Now he encountered the frenetic chaos at the scene and decided he needed to go inside and help. His father, Russell, a highway department employee and rescue squad volunteer, "had a fit about me going into the cave, but I told him I knew it pretty well, so he let me go," Milton said.

Inside, Milton saw the familiar criss-cross passageways, most of them pretty narrow with an occasional good-sized room where limestone passages intersected. Some of those areas could accommodate a standing adult. "Many of the passages only went twenty or thirty feet and then became too small for an adult to squeeze through." He wondered if the boys could have gotten further in one of these tight passages, encountered a problem, and were now out of reach of adult searchers. While inside, he came across a young Quincy caver who had gotten lost in the confusing cave system, so Milton showed him the way out.

Milton desperately wanted to find the boys. He was friends with Fred Hoag, the boys' older brother, from their time as members of Boy Scout Troop 112 at Stowell School. "I figured if the boys were trapped they probably could last three days without water," Milton reasoned. As he moved slowly through a tight passage, his mind raced. *What the hell is happening? This is a damn tragedy,* he thought. During the next few hours, Milton explored several passages, finding no evidence of the boys or anything that would hint of trouble. "I stayed until midnight and went home, but lots of people stayed to continue searching overnight."

***

Bill Boltinghouse was a senior at Hannibal High School and looked forward to graduating soon. He worked at Sandy's, a local drive-in fast food restaurant and would be joining the Air Force in a few weeks. On the evening of May 10, Bill had received a telephone call at home from a cousin, Carl Nelson, who worked as a dispatcher for the Hannibal Police Department. "He asked if I knew the Hoag boys and whether I'd heard they were missing and lost in the cave," Boltinghouse related. Surprised to hear the news, he quickly drove to the Southside search location.

When Bill arrived, the scene was growing increasingly chaotic, with more people entering the caves unsupervised. Bill borrowed a local caver's helmet and carbide lamp to illuminate the way, but once he was thirty yards into the cave, the lamp went out leaving Bill in the deepest, most surreal blackness ever. "It was more penetrating than any darkness you've ever experienced. Fortunately, another volunteer near me filled the carbide tank on my helmet, and I was back in business."

The carbide helmet lights used by cavers in the 1960s utilized calcium carbide nuggets which, when mixed with water, released combustible acetylene gas that gave off light once ignited. A full load of carbide would keep a caver going for three to four hours. The lamps also produced heat that helped cavers to stay warm in cool cave environments.

This was Boltinghouse's first time in the cave. He knew Craig Dowell was an inquisitive boy, so it didn't surprise him to learn Craig was among the missing. Being a citizens band and ham radio enthusiast, Bill quickly recognized that communications would play an important role during the search. Already, precious time was being lost as rescue personnel relied on runners to send messages out for equipment and water. As the rescuers toiled into the night, Bill returned home and began gathering his radio gear together.

At the search headquarters at Southside Christian Church, adjacent to the Highway 79 construction site, Boltinghouse quickly set up his base station and antenna so the search personnel could have efficient operational communications. A radio enthusiast from nearby Quincy pitched in to help.

Bill powered up the base station, adjusted the volume, and keyed the microphone. "This is KPH9292, how do you read?" "We hear you loud and clear," replied a search worker at the Murphy's Cave site three blocks north. They were in business. "The gear really helped because they no longer had to send runners back and forth with messages," Boltinghouse said. "The cavers had no way to talk to us while in the caves because the earth and rock absorbed the radio frequency radiation emitted by the walkie talkies. So cavers talked to people near the cave entrances who would radio messages between the search personnel and the church headquarters."

***

Coincidentally, in nearby Quincy, Illinois, Al Viar, then twenty-three, was at home hosting the regular Wednesday night meeting of his local caving club when the phone rang about nine p.m. Quincy police were calling, desperate to find cavers who might help search for the missing Hannibal boys. The officer had a short message. "We've got to get those kids out of the cave, can you help?" Viar quickly consented and several caving club members gathered their gear.

Viar, who worked at a local manufacturer of perforated steel beams, had been caving for years, exploring numerous local and regional caves, including local Burton Cave and the Mark Twain and Cameron Caves near Hannibal, as well as other major caves around the country. As caving grew in popularity as a hobby, Viar had joined the Quincy caving club, which included several adults and some teens, and was later elected club president. "At one point, we had forty cavers in the Quincy area," Viar said.

Viar and others from his caving group arrived in Hannibal after ten p.m and immediately joined the frantic search underway in Murphy's Cave. "At first we were confused by all the string running everywhere through the passages to the entrance that had been put in place by the rescue squad members. Seeing all the string, I wondered why they had called us," he mused.

The Quincyans found the search slow going as they moved stooped over through the narrow passageways. "It's a big cave with many spurs in many different directions," Viar said, "and we found several areas of ceiling breakdown." He knew it would take time to explore those breakdowns in the days ahead.

***

In nearby Palmyra, a 10:30 p.m. phone call shattered the quiet at Lynnie Hoag's house. The nineteen-year-old had just fallen asleep when the desperate call from her mother, Helen, snapped her awake. "Mom said, 'The boys disappeared. Come over here.'" Lynnie dressed and departed for the fifteen-minute drive to the Southside neighborhood, trying to make sense of what was unfolding.

Unaware the caves had been reopened during construction, she was stunned to learn the boys had been exploring underground. While driving, Lynnie's mind filled with possible scenarios. Were they trapped and hurt underground? She knew her brothers well; they were boys who loved to hitchhike and would readily accept a ride from a total stranger. Had they been kidnapped? Her eyes grew moist as she pondered the possibilities.

Lynnie soon joined her shocked family at the Murphy's Cave location, now a bustling beehive of activity. "There were all these people rushing in every direction, and bright lights were erected by the cave. I felt like I was dreaming, like I'd never woken up. I was just numb with emotion, having never experienced anything like that," Lynnie explained.

Family and friends were helping with the search, and Lynnie was desperate to assist, too. "But Mom and Dad never let us girls go. They felt it would be too hard on us if something bad was to be found," she said.

To complicate matters, the sky opened up, unleashing a heavy downpour that fell during the late evening. The Murphy's Cave and roadcut areas had turned into muddy messes, perhaps increasing the risk of a collapse of the cave ceilings or entrances along the hillsides.

The Speleological Society of America's incident report captured the desperation of that first night's search before any experienced expert cave specialists had arrived on the scene: "Far into the night, the Mark Twain Rescue Squad, aided by townspeople, crisscrossed themselves in Murphy's Cave, without locating the boys."

Hannibal was birthing a painful new chapter of its history. Families and townspeople were worried, desperate for any reassurance. America's Hometown would soon make history as the site of the largest, most extensive cave search in US history.

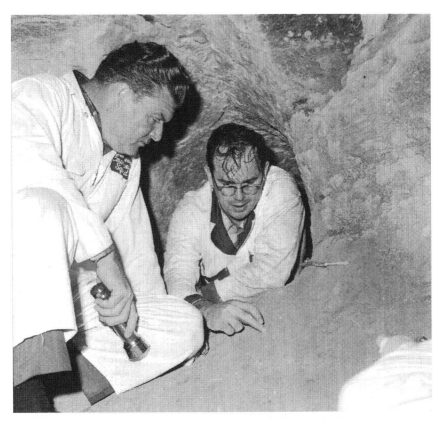

Two Mark Twain Emergency Squad members discuss next moves in complex Murphy's Cave. Photo courtesy Hannibal Courier-Post.

Chapter 3

Other Lost Children

"It was not our time to die."

Boys Lost in Cave

"The avenues are said to be very narrow and torturous. They intersect each other after the manner of streets and blocks."

Excerpt from 1873 *Hannibal Courier* newspaper story.

Incredibly, three adventurous boys believed lost in the Hannibal caves was not a unique, one-off emergency. Extensive research has revealed two similar incidents that occurred during the previous ninety-four years.

We travel back to early April 1873. A major battle in the American Indian Wars was soon to be fought, pitting westward-expanding colonizers and federal government forces against the native peoples. The St. Louis Board of Education launched the nation's first kindergarten class. Henry Rose prepared to unveil his new invention—barbed wire—at an Illinois county fair. And Levi Strauss had submitted a patent application for using copper rivets on denim work pants.

In Hannibal, with a population of 10,125 residents, progress also marched onward. City fathers announced the inaugural run of the first streetcar, a horse-drawn vehicle. Resident Charles McDaniel, a pioneer in the development of telephone technology, was planning to wire the town and bring phone service to Hannibalians in just six years. Lumbering was the dominant industry, providing many jobs for townspeople who processed logs—floated downriver from Minnesota and Wisconsin—into lumber transported by rail to build the rapidly expanding American West.

In South Hannibal, near the spot where the Hoag and Dowell boys would one day explore cave passages, townspeople had their own cave search and rescue mission underway. The focus was the same cave complex that would capture the national spotlight during the desperate, race-against-time 1967 search.

Just twenty-five years after Samuel Clemens left Hannibal and his job as a Mississippi riverboat hand, five boys ages nine to thirteen went missing in a newly uncovered cave near the intersection of Walnut Street and what is now named Birch Street. Much construction was underway in Hannibal, so the quarries were busily excavating stone and fire clay needed for streets and foundations. After blasting the east side of Ide's Hill, quarry workers discovered the gateway to a subterranean world.

The following verbatim account of the rescue is from the April 5, 1873 *Hannibal Courier* newspaper.

Five Boys Lost in a Cave

In quarrying in South Hannibal, Missouri, a cave was recently discovered by the workmen. An exploring expedition was organized by five boys, whose ages ranged from nine to thirteen years. Providing themselves with pieces of candle an inch or two in length, which were all lighted at once, the little torchlight procession marched into the cave. Other boys at the same time went in a short distance and returned. The five were not missed by their parents until a late hour in the evening when they were informed by the lads who

40

had entered with them that they had gone into the cave at ten o'clock in the morning, since which time they had not seen them.

The alarm that five boys were lost in the cave drew a vast crowd around its mouth, among whom were the fathers, mothers, brothers and sisters of the lost ones. Several parties immediately entered the cave in search of them, but all returned without a trace of the lost children.

About eleven o'clock at night a party of five was organized, who entered the cave with the determination to do or die. In order not to lose their way, they unwound a ball of twine as they proceeded. In this way six balls of twine were used up, when they discovered tracks near a rift or fissure in the rocks, barely large enough to admit the body of the smallest of the party. He squeezed himself through it, and going some distance, he called out, receiving no answer. He penetrated still further, and called again, when he thought he heard a faint response, and called again. When he thought he heard a faint response he thrust forward the bull's-eye lantern which he carried, and proceeding in a like manner some distance further he heard a voice exclaim: "Oh, I see a light!" and he knew the lost were found. When found, they were in a crevice in the rock, seeking a larger place where they could all lie down and sleep together.

The joy consequent upon their deliverance almost overcame them. The searching party emerged from the cave about one o'clock at night. The midnight air was made glad by the shouts of joy which greeted their appearance in the outer world, while parents clasped their darlings to their hearts, their eyes streaming with tears, and their lips uttering prayers of thanksgiving to God for their safe deliverance.

The boys stated that their candles went out, and they groped around in the darkness to find the way back, during which time the youngest of the little party was taken sick with a severe chill and lay down. They rubbed him vigorously and succeeded in restoring him, after which they proceeded on their search for the entrance. After wandering for hours and their efforts proving vain, they sat down and cried. Drying their tears, they encouraged each other with the hope that the boys who entered the cave part of the way with them would tell their parents, upon which a search would be instituted and in fact, to this lack of courage on the part of their comrades who felt sheepish enough when they retreated amid the jeers of the bolder boys they saved their lives.

Some days ago we mentioned the fact that the mouth of an extensive cave had been unearthed in a stone quarry in South Hannibal. Since its discovery it has been a favorite resort for boys who have daily made exploration of the vast subterranean labyrinth. Yesterday, however, an expedition was organized to explore the cave, the adventures of which are destined to give the newly discovered cavern local fame and history that will not soon be forgotten.

The lads composing the party were five in number as follows: Dana McDaniel, aged 13 years; Robert

Gardner, aged 13 years; Harry Hunstock, aged 12 years; Fred Crout, aged 12 years; Clarence Crout, aged 9 years.

The boys entered the cave about 10 o'clock yesterday morning, each provided with a small bit of candle two or three inches long, all burning at once, the torchlight procession marched through the silent depths very gaily and happily, looking for curiosities and searching for strange scenes. Some other boys entered the cave about the same time, followed them a short distance and returned. Our heroes however had determined on a thorough exploration of the unknown cavern, and went on, and on, through the winding rifts and fissures of the rocks until their candles had nearly burned out and when they attempted to return they found themselves in the condition of the five foolish virgins, and were left in total darkness to grope and crawl amid the mud and dirt, sharp stones and jagged rocks.

None of the parents of the boys missed them until late in the evening, and upon inquiry of some of their playmates it was ascertained they had gone into the cave at the hour named since which time they had not been heard or seen. About 7 o'clock last evening the alarm was given that five boys were lost in the cave, and in a short time a large crowd, estimated at 500 to 600 persons, were gathered about its mouth, among them the fathers, mothers, brothers, sisters, relations and friends of the lost children, all in terrible suspense and shedding many bitter tears, and their feelings during the long and painful hours of search can be better imagined than here described. Searching parties were organized to explore the cavern, and as they would return with no tidings of the lost ones, many a parent's heart was filled with anguish, and all manner of horrid deaths were conjured up as having befallen the little fellows who were thus buried alive. Small persons were in demand to enter the cave and look for the lost ones as, owing to the formation of the rifts, it is impossible for a large person to squeeze through in many places, and money was freely offered for volunteers to prosecute the search, as well as a reward for the one who should bring out the boys.

Several parties returned from the cavern without gaining any trace of the boys and the hours of suspense seemed like days—midnight was approaching and still a large and anxious crowd stood around the dread opening and among those present were many ladies. Candles were furnished in abundance while balls of twine were provided and led in through the windings of the cave to afford a guide for those who entered to return. Charles McDaniel also took in with him in his first exploration a paint pot and brush with which he marked arrows on the rocks pointing towards the mouth of the cave. These precautions enabled those who entered to readily find the way out.

The Successful Party

Shortly after 11 o'clock last night a party of five was organized for the next effort, composed of the following persons: Charles McDaniel, Lafayette Robison, Jim Turner, Tom Ford and Everett McDaniel. They entered and followed up the twine, six balls of which had been used in tracing the windings of this cave. Here they discovered the tracks of the lost boys, who had crawled through a very small crevice. Charles McDaniel here took the lead and after crawling some distance through a rift just large enough to admit his body, he called out, when from the dark, unknown depths beyond he heard a faint response which he says sounded like the squeak of a mouse. He crawled on still further and called again, when a nearer and louder response greeted him; again he crawled forward lighting up the darkness beyond him with a bull's-eye light which he carried in his hand, when he heard a voice exclaim "Oh, I see a light!" Soon he caught sight of the little fellows all huddled together in an opening between two vast rocks, one under them and one above, with barely room for to lie stretched out, but too low for them to even stand on their hands and knees, while in width in most places it was barely sufficient to admit of the passage of one at a time. As he came near them, and the boys caught sight of his face, Dana McDaniel exclaimed, "Oh thank God there is my brother" and the little fellows shed tears of joy at their deliverance from their long and painful immurement. They were completely exhausted and when the welcome voice came to their ears through the awful darkness, the little fellows were looking for an open space where they could lie down together and sleep. Charley provided them with candles and finding a place sufficiently large, allowed them to pass him, he bringing up the rear and encouraging the lads to work their way out, as the joy of their deliverance seemed to quite overcome them, and caused them to feel like sinking down in their tracks. It was

45

five minutes past 12, midnight, when they were discovered, and at ten minutes before 1 o'clock Lafayette Robison emerged from the cave, leading the way and announcing that the boys had been found, were all safe and sound, and on their way out. They whole party soon emerged from the cave, and the shouts of joy that greeted the rescuers and the rescued was so hearty and loud that it was heard in nearly all parts of the city, and rang out on the midnight air as though a great victory had been won. Fathers and mothers clasped their children to their hearts while tears of joy and gratitude rolled down their cheeks.

During the wanderings of these youthful Cimmerii in the darkness of the cavern, the younger Crout was taken with a chill and laid down quite sick. His companions staid [sic] by him like little heroes, covering him with their coats and rubbing his limbs until they got him warmed up and able to proceed.

In conversation with one of the boys today, he informed us that after they had struggled for a long time to find their way out and had become thoroughly disheartened, they all sat down together and took a big cry, bewailing their fate and filled with apprehensions that they would never again gaze upon the blessed light of day. Finally, they dried their tears and reasoned together, and cheered each other with hopes of deliverance. Their abiding faith was in the love of their fathers and mothers - they know that they would be missed - and they believed that the boys who had followed them in for a short distance and returned, would give information of their whereabouts. In this they were correct, and now that they are free again they should resolve to be very good boys, to make amends for the untold anguish they so unwittingly inflicted upon their loving parents.

Their clothes were completely worn out, and the little fellows covered with mud and dirt. They all unite in saying that they have seen all they desire of the South Hannibal Cave, and advise boys generally to keep out of it. Charlie McDaniel's shoes were worn down to his toes and his clothes were worn threadbare, caused by having to crawl so much.

A later newspaper account, which erroneously reported the number of boys missing as three rather than five, offered a more complete early glimpse of one of Missouri's most complex maze caves.

... the excavation of shale debris for fire clay revealed a crevice at the east end of the hill abutting Fifth Street [now Birch Street] in south Hannibal. Three little boys went in there and at night they were missing. By chance another lad was able to tell what had become of them. A rescue party went in with a cord for a clue in returning. About ten o'clock the boys were found. They had also relied on a string clue, but the passages were so crooked they had crossed their route without knowing it and when they tried to return they took the wrong course of the twine. The rescue cord proved to be about a fourth of a mile long. The opening was closed and no further exploration has been attempted. The avenues are said to be very narrow and torturous. They intersect each other after the manner of streets and blocks.

Across time, the dark narrow passages had beckoned children who seemed powerless to resist this world beneath their feet. The early discovery of this cave by curious pioneer boys not only foreshadowed future disappearances, but also the daunting challenge modern-day cavers and search and rescue personnel would face in 1967, as they crept through the complex of narrow passages that is south Hannibal's geologic underbelly.

The cave was named Murphy's Cave, after the property owner Cornelius Murphy who operated a grocery store with business partner Clarence Lampton at the northwest corner of Walnut and Birch streets. The cave was sealed, but that would not be the end of the childhood hazard.

Decades later, in the 1960s, the cave was mapped by experienced cavers Don Myers, Don Nicholson, Jim Clark, Frank Alexander, Dwight Weaver and others who compiled the more complete portrait of Murphy's Cave that would be used by cavers in 1967. These early cave mappers found an intricate maze cave, among the largest in Missouri. It was a confusing matrix of intersecting passages that stretched for nearly 9,500 feet beneath Hannibal's Southside. Myers' cave map (see photo section) loosely resembled the organized grid of streets in a modern city or town. But the passages were all nearly identical in appearance, which made the potential for getting lost very high. An explorer moving along one passage may come to a branch and discover three or four others sprouting from the route being traversed. Taking any one of these passages, the cave explorer soon would come to another series of passages branching off yet again. "It's like an underground tree," as one caver explained, "the passages being the trunk, limbs, and branches, and it goes on and on like this for nearly two miles of passages."

***

We now move ahead to June 1961, an era of growing international turmoil and cultural change in America. President John F. Kennedy, in office only five months, was already embroiled in heated talks with Soviet Premier Nikita Khrushchev. The Cold War pushed the unthinkable threat of a nuclear nightmare upon the national psyche, and families found themselves having dinner table conversations about whether to build a fallout shelter in the backyard. American country singer Patsy Kline nearly lost her life in a head-on car collision in Nashville. The Sony Corporation made its first public stock offering in the United States at $1.75 a share. The number one song in America was Ricky Nelson's "Travelin' Man." And on television, *You Bet Your Life*, a thirty-minute game show hosted by comedian Groucho Marx, was broadcast for the last time.

On Hannibal's bucolic Southside, now fully developed with streets lined with tidy, modern bungalows, many with white picket fences, a summer of discovery was unfolding for the Owen boys whose family had recently moved from the country into town. Ed, Ron, and Billy were making new friends and exploring the nearby wooded hills, rock quarries and caves.

Their home, located at 710 Birch, sat only a few blocks north of the hilly neighborhood that later would be transformed during Highway 79 construction. And just catycorner across the street from the Owen home, hidden in the hillside weeds, was the old entrance to Murphy's Cave. Soon, the haunting landmark would again make an indelible, enduring impression upon a group of twentieth century teens... a chilling, unforgettable experience they would carry for life.

The Owen brothers' close call in Murphy Cave is a memory so vivid they still get a chill down the spine as they discuss the resurrected memories. "It's as if the incident happened only yesterday," they say.

Today, Ron Owen, a painter by trade, lives in Quincy, Illinois. Ed Owen lives in semi-retirement with his family in Jacksonville, Illinois, seventy miles east of Hannibal. Ed's avocations are more sedate these days; he enjoys painting scenic landscapes, playing the saxophone, and participating in church activities with his family. Despite the many years that have passed, Ed and Ron still clearly remember their childhood adventures, one riveting day in particular.

"I was recently telling my neighbor about being lost in the cave. It's something that doesn't ever leave your memory," Ed explained on a crisp fall day. He escorts a visitor into his art studio and takes a seat to tell his caving story. "I'm grateful I'm here today. It could have been us lost in those caves," he said.

Ed Owen, left, and brother Ron outside the Murphy's Cave entrance they entered in June 1961. Photo by John Wingate.

It was one of those perfect sunny June days in 1961, Ed remembers, a carefree time not long after school had ended when summer lay ahead full of promise, leisure, and adventure. Having recently moved to Hannibal, Ed, Ron, and Billy Owen were game for daily explorations of their neighborhood and the countryside near the southern edge of town.

"We'd just moved to Hannibal when I was in ninth grade," Ed explained, "and it was culture shock for me. I went from a two-room country school to a big, modern junior high." Slowly making new friends, the Owen brothers became acquainted with their new neighborhood in historic Hannibal. "We'd just go around looking for things to do—climb Lover's Leap, monkey around along the Mississippi riverbank, climb trees. I was adventurous and liked being outdoors. Dad worked at the cement plant, and we were always exploring the huge limestone quarry down at the plant site. We'd find bobcat tracks, big crinoid fossils. It was a great, fun way to spend a day," Ed recalled.

"Often we'd get a ride down to Mark Twain Cave and explore it," Ed said. "That cave is taller and wider than Murphy's Cave." One day Archie Cameron, the owner of Mark Twain Cave, asked the Owen boys if they wanted to see another cave nearby with some really neat features. "Yeah! We were all for that," Ed recalled. "The cave had a locked entrance, so Archie escorted us inside and we walked around for nearly an hour."

Discovered by Cameron in 1925, and now open as a show cave, Cameron Cave is the third largest maze cave in the Northern Hemisphere with a network of passages extending 24,390 feet horizontally. It is larger than nearby Mark Twain Cave, with twice the passages in its eighteen acres. "I remember it had some neat quartz crystal projections and mineral 'falls' features (Buttermilk Falls) where running water over millions of years' time had made an impression in the rock," Ed remembered. "When we left, he made sure to lock the gate so no one could get in there." Ed instinctively knew a large cave like that could be a dangerous place.

"That summer," Ed explained, "we were constantly looking for something like this to do. So when Steve Borden, one of the neighbor boys, came down to the house and said, *'Hey Ed, you've got to see this. We found a cave up on the hill!'* well, we were all set for adventure!"

This particular entrance to Murphy's Cave, rediscovered by generations of youngsters since its initial discovery in the 1870s, is located a short distance up a wooded slope, immediately north of Walnut Street on the west side of Birch Street. For Ed, his brother Ron, and their friends, Steve Borden and Kevin Foster, it was an exciting new discovery at the beginning of their endless summer. For the restless teens, the adventures of Tom Sawyer and Huckleberry Finn were coming to life in *their* era.

"It was the first time any of us had ever seen this cave entrance," Ed said. "A fifty-gallon barrel was stuck in it, and rain had washed away the dirt around it over the years. The barrel was loose enough that we could pull it out of there, and that's when we saw the cave opening."

By now, the boys were overtaken by such a frenzy of discovery they could hardly contain themselves. Such adventure, and so close to home. They lined up, pushing and jostling impatiently as Ed went first, jumping down into the cave entrance, quickly followed by the others. The youngest Owen brother, Billy, had followed his brothers to the site, but after initially jumping into the cave he got spooked by the dark, claustrophobic passages and climbed back out.

"Some caves you can walk right into them from ground level, but with this one you had to go down into it first," Ed said. "You dropped down vertically about three feet, then you could slip into a passageway and it's open. You could stand up in some of the passages," he added.

"It was like a *real* discovery, but we had no idea how huge it was, so were curious to find out. We later heard a story about a guy who'd gone into Murphy's Cave with plenty of food and water. He was supposedly in there for three days, and finally smelled fresh air and emerged from an opening in a grassy field way out on Fulton Avenue, southwest of Hannibal. He had to have gone at least three-quarters of a mile in that cave. That's a *lot* of distance underground," Ed explained.

Despite the boys' impulsive enthusiasm, further exploration of Murphy's had to be postponed because it was late in the day. Ed, Ron, Steve and Kevin reluctantly made plans to meet up the next day and launch a full exploration of their new discovery. "Since it was evening," Ed explained, "I told them we'd all meet at the cave tomorrow. If you've got balls of string, bring 'em. Flashlights, candles, matches, bring everything you can."

After supper that evening, the Owen brothers sat on the front porch of their modest home and discussed tomorrow's plans in hushed whispers out of reach of parental ears. The twilight sky, streaked with brilliant purples and reds, soon gave way overhead to the glistening crown of the Milky Way. Gazing up at a sliver of the new moon, the Owen brothers recalled President Kennedy's announcement just a few weeks earlier on May 25, 1961: "I believe that this nation should commit itself to achieving the goal, before this decade is out, of landing a man on the moon and returning him safely to Earth."

We're living in a bold era of exploration, Ed thought. And it's our time to become explorers, too.

Below the grand, celestial tapestry overhead lurked the deeply-shadowed, overgrown hillside up the street, its underworld beckoning. The boys grew tired as blinking lightning bugs broke the darkness intermittently in the still, humid night air.

The next morning, the Owen boys jumped out of bed, dressed, and gathered around the formica table. After wolfing down breakfast, they raced off to meet their pals at the cave to discuss their plans. "Someone brought a big ball of heavy string, so we tied that off outside of the cave," Ed recalls. "I knew it was a mixed up, confusing cave with a lot of different passages, so we knew the tendency to get lost in there would be great. So I told the guys, 'We'll take string in there and follow that, then we can follow it back out.'"

The boys agreed to the plan and proceeded to enter Murphy's Cave single file. As they cautiously moved down the first narrow passageway, one of the boys unwound the string, surrendering a foot at a time. They discussed whether they might find some creatures in the cave but were soon disappointed. "There were no bats or snakes or insects of any kind that we could see. Only some small puddles of water from seepage," Ron explained.

On that day, it appeared the only evident life in Murphy's Cave was one curious species—prone to act before thinking—young, impulsive Homo sapien teenagers.

The teens moved along the illuminated path, steadying themselves against the cool Louisiana Limestone walls, their sneakers occasionally scuffing the damp, hard-packed buff-colored clay floor. Each boy had a flashlight, which they agreed to rotate to avoid wasting precious battery power, but no one had thought to bring any water or food. They had a candle and matches along, but they dreaded the thought of having to rely on just a candle flame if trouble developed and they ran out of battery power. None of the boys had told anyone their plans to explore the cave, so they were on their own if something went wrong. But what could go amiss on such a glorious day?

Most of the time, the boys walked upright as they visually absorbed the cavescape. Occasionally they were forced to hunch down in areas with a lower ceiling and drop to their hands and knees to crawl through a few narrow spots in the cave. No one seemed worried. *This is great fun,* Ron thought.

But their adventurous spirit was soon dampened by reality. "Well, lo and behold," Ed said, "we got way back in there, probably several hundred feet, and ran out of string. That's how far back in there we were, many *hundreds* of feet. But we weren't really worried at that point. We felt pretty sure of ourselves, all of us confident we could eventually find our way back out."

The teenagers then made a significant lapse in judgement. They decided to continue on their subterranean journey, no longer marking their path in this complex maze cave, where every passage largely looks the same in monotonous shades of tan. The cave now seemed to close in on them with each step taken; the boys felt like they were on another planet in that dark and shadowy world below their serene neighborhood. Still, they pressed onward for a few more hours, each passageway offering up three, four or more other branching routes. The boys took a new course and were soon faced with more route options. The foursome kept moving, this way and that, ever onward, unaware of the perilous situation developing, not thinking about the struggle they would face once they reversed course to begin the long trek back out of that complicated maze cave.

There were exciting landmarks for the novice spelunkers to explore and study along the way. "We'd shine our lights and see crevices along the floor in some areas," said Ed. "You'd shine a light down in them and couldn't see the bottom, so I don't know how deep it might be. We were scared we might step into one of them. They weren't too wide, anywhere from eight inches to a foot wide. But a caver could easily twist an ankle if they stepped in one, and that would be bad."

The teens carefully made their way around the crevices, but were suddenly stopped cold in their tracks, feet frozen to the cave floor. Ahead, the ever-unfolding passageway had abruptly ended. The boys gazed upward, Ed's lead flashlight illuminating a portion of the ceiling that had collapsed, piling up at an angle and blocking the narrow cave passage. "Oh man! Look at that!"

The teens grew wide-eyed as they looked down to see something protruding from the heap. "At first glance I thought it was a bone, but then realized that it was a wooden handle of some kind," Ed said. "We wondered if there were people under there," he added. *Was somebody buried under or behind that rubble?* "We stared at it for a long while, but I'd never heard of anyone missing in the area, so I didn't venture to dig it out. We just figured someone left a shovel there, and the dirt fell in on it later. So we backed out and went another way."

By now, Ron, age fifteen and a year younger than Ed, was growing tired, his flashlight dimming quickly. The underground chill penetrated his slender frame. "We were still strung out in a line," Ron said, "one behind the other. After a while, I said, 'I think I'm just going to wait here. My flashlight batteries are getting kind of low, and I'm tired of crawling around and everything.' The others told me to stay put and they'd be back."

The three other boys moved on, their voices quickly trailing off as they rounded a corner. Ron settled in and sat alone in his muddied trousers, his back against the cool limestone wall deep inside the chilly cave. His flashlight was now emitting such a faint glow he kept it off most of the time to conserve what little battery power remained, turning it on only occasionally as a reassuring but weak beacon to cut the suffocating darkness. Every fear within him seemed to rise up, overtaking the happy, adventurous thoughts that had once occupied his mind. "It was scary," Ron said. "I realized I should have stayed with the other three, then it started getting a little spooky. I sat there for a long time." *They're not coming back soon. I wonder what's taking them so long.*

"I was fifteen and a half, and I waited alone probably three hours, maybe longer. That doesn't sound like long, but it is when you're in *complete* cave darkness." Ron longed for the other boys to return. "I did a little praying to God, it was that serious. Real fear. I thought that if I didn't get out of there I'd be dead. Without a flashlight I'd have to eventually try to feel my way out, an impossible feat in total darkness, I figured."

In the inky darkness, Ron briskly rubbed his bare arms to generate a little warmth, raw fear caught in his throat as his stomach tightened in a knot. *I don't like this,* he thought.

Meanwhile, Ed and his two friends were advancing continuously. "Our flashlights weren't as bright, and we'd been proceeding forward on our own for another few hours at least," Ed said. "Then we decided to turn back, and that's when we realized we were lost. We got pretty nervous fast."

The boys thought they had a clear sense of the route, but they didn't fully appreciate, at the time, that they were in a maze cave. "One passage goes along and turns into several passages branching off from it," Ed said. "This pattern just keeps repeating. It's incredible, like being in the middle of a thousand-square-mile corn field and thinking it's going to be easy to find your way out.

"I believe it's nearly impossible [for a novice] to find their way out of a maze cave. You can be in there wandering around for days and starve to death. It's just that simple. And that's why they tell people not to go into caves without professional training and equipment. It's easy to go in, but getting back out can be challenging," Ed explained.

The boys worried they'd mistakenly walk in a huge circle, wasting precious time and ever-dwindling battery power, without ever actually finding their way out. They had no desire to spend the next day or days in a chilly cave with no light, no food, no water or warm clothing. *No desire to die in a cave whose entrance is a mere one hundred yards from my house*, Ed worried.

"We couldn't just keep walking blindly," explained Ed, "so we pulled our thoughts together and tried to stay calm. As we reversed our course, we had to be certain of our movements. We could make no mistakes. If we didn't see footprints or any markings on the hard, clay surface... if it didn't look right, I stopped immediately, turned around, and we went back and took another route."

Occasionally, the boys saw evidence they'd passed through a passage earlier, so they'd go back down that route. "When you know you're lost it seems like all your abilities and wits are really enhanced. You certainly can't panic. And you can't yell for help in there, either. I'll bet your voice would only carry fifteen feet. With so many bends in the short passages, and all the rock and dirt, it would just kill the sound. It's like yelling into a towel in your cupped hands. Sound just doesn't travel very far. I just thanked the good Lord he gave me common sense to keep a cool head that day," Ed said.

Back in another area of Murphy's, young Ron's mood was quickly ebbing toward despair. He'd sat alone in the dark for three hours, his only companion the sounds of his own breathing and heartbeat breaking the thick silence. Suddenly, his ears caught something distant and muffled. *What's that?* "I thought I heard something, muted voices, and then after a while I saw some flickering light and I thought, *Oh, it's them, finally!*"

The boys soon let out a cheer, thrilled to be reunited. "When I finally saw Ron it was like getting air after not being able to breathe," Ed exclaimed. "I was thinking thank you, Lord!" After a few backslaps, Ed asked Ron if he'd found the way out. "'No, I've been waiting here the whole time for you guys.' They thought *I'd* found the way out and had come back for *them*," Ron explained.

Together, the four boys boldly pressed onward, rededicated to a shared objective and soon to be blessed by good fortune. Step by step, single file, they carefully made their way along the uneven clay and limestone passages, avoiding the crevices, hoping each step was bringing them closer to freedom. A long hour passed as they nervously traveled through Murphy's.

Suddenly their hearts jumped and spirits soared, smiles replacing the concern that had etched their faces most of the day. Ahead on the packed cave floor, barely illuminated by their last failing flashlight, lay the end of the string—their tether to home.

"In another thirty minutes or so we were out of the cave, and when I saw daylight, smelled fresh air and felt the warm sun, I felt true happiness," Ron exclaimed.

Ed agreed. "It was a gift from God that got us out of there. I was so glad to be out of that cave. I think I made a vow that I'd never go in there again. I've never seen such a maze. It was just all over, and we surely didn't see all of it. My, my," he said, shaking his head in amazement. "Looking back, we were boys who acted too impulsively, we were overly brave, so foolish to take that risk, really. It was not our time to die, and I do think we could have died in there."

Even today, Ron is astonished at their good fortune that fateful June day in 1961. "We just had cheap flashlights, common dime-store lights at that time. No water, no food, we hadn't told anyone we were going in the cave. We were just boys, teenagers, prone to adventure."

The four young cavers had entered Murphy's Cave mid-morning, and by the time they finally found their way out it was nearly seven o'clock in the evening. The Owen boys ran home, quickly changed out of their muddy, wet clothes and a few days later told their mother they'd gone into the cave, failing to mention they had been lost most of the day. They gratefully accepted the stern reprimand she meted out, her finger wagging in their faces, knowing they would never set foot in the cave again. *Yes ma'am, never again. EVER! We promise.*

For Ron Owen, the hours alone in the darkness took a lasting toll. "After that, I always slept with a nightlight on, even now. That complete darkness, all alone, is a memory I'll never forget."

Murphy's Cave had surrendered these boys, but in six short years the cave would make headlines worldwide, as a shocked community would again heroically conduct a massive race-against-time search—the largest cave search in US history—for three lost boys in America's hometown.

Cavers at two early entrances into Murphy's Cave. Photo Courtesy Quincy Herald-Whig.

Chapter 4

Race Against Time

"When I was a boy and I would see scary things in the news. My mother would say to me: 'Look for the helpers. You will always find people who are helping.'"

Fred Rogers, host of Mister Rogers' Neighborhood on PBS

Southsider Steve Sederwall, then fourteen, arose on May 11, donned blue jeans and a blue button-down shirt, and sleepily settled at the kitchen table for breakfast. The leather-cased transistor radio, an ever-present fixture on the countertop, had just carried KHMO-AM's morning newscast for his mother, Barbara, to hear. The atmosphere in the room seemed suddenly heavy as Steve entered the room. Barbara slid Steve's usual platter of eggs on toast before him, but quickly turned away, her eyes glistening with tears.

Still unaware of the news, Steve quietly finished his breakfast, gathered his books and prepared to depart for the bus stop. "Mom gave me a long hug goodbye and whispered 'I love you,' but she wouldn't turn me loose, so I wondered what was going on," Sederwall remembered.

Later, he realized the long hug was one of gratitude. "She was thanking God it was not her boys lost in a cave."

***

As Hannibalians stirred that day, they found themselves in a strange new reality as they vacillated between rollercoaster feelings of shock, hope and despair. Most believed the boys would be quickly found and life would soon return to normal. But privately, many feared the worst.

News of the missing boys spread like wildfire Thursday at Hannibal Junior High School. Students, who just twenty-four hours earlier were light-hearted and looking forward to the approaching end of the school year, were now stunned by the unfolding emergency, shuffling through the halls between classes and offering as much encouragement as they could muster to classmates.

"You can imagine the shock. It was really spooky, such a feeling of disbelief," said Gary Rush who was in eighth grade at the time and a good friend of Joel Hoag. "Everybody knew each other so we were just heartsick. It was really surreal." Rush and other Southside kids were a tight pack of adventurous youngsters who often played in the nearby hills. "Joel loved the outdoors, and Billy was always tagging along with us."

***

Early Thursday morning, Bill Boltinghouse jumped back into the cave search, exploring Murphy's and another cave located around the hillside, closer to Bear Creek, the Southside's defining northern border. When he heard the whistle of an approaching train on the nearby tracks, he held his breath, not knowing what to expect and waited as the rumbling vibrations moved through the earth like a lit fuse. Suddenly, debris rained down from the cave ceiling, partially burying Boltinghouse who now found himself needing rescue by his search partners. They quickly removed the loose debris from his sprawled body and stayed with him until he regained his composure. It was a close call he and the other cavers would not soon forget.

Up to five teams of three men each were now inside the cave, often forced to crawl on their hands and knees in small passages of diminishing diameters and some very tight squeezes. If only they could will themselves smaller and thinner. In some areas of the cave, they walked on the walls because the floor of the passages was too narrow for their feet. They made arduously slow progress in this difficult, subterranean universe where everything was hard and unforgiving.

In St. Louis, one hundred miles to the south, Conway Christensen, Chief of the Hondo Underground Rescue Team (HURT) had been following the search with increasing concern, after hearing a morning radio report. Christensen also served as vice president of the Speleological Society of America (SSA), a new Virginia-based cave rescue organization that had been established by Virginian William Karras the previous October. Karras was a controversial figure because of his rift with the well-established National Speleological Society over the priority that should be placed on cave rescue as an organizational focus. As Karras, a vice president at a Virginia manufacturing firm, directed his attention to Hannibal, he was keen on enhancing the visibility of the SSA and reinforcing the importance and necessity of cave rescue services.

On Thursday, May 11, Christensen placed his rescue team on alert after talking with Karras who also served as chief of the National Capital Cave Rescue Team. The two cave rescue teams had functioned well together during previous cave emergencies in other states.

By noon, the Hannibal Police Department had formally requested assistance from HURT. "Several grotto members, including some students from St. Mary's High School in St. Louis, took leave and got their gear together, and we departed Thursday afternoon," said Christensen, an employee of McDonnell-Douglas, a major aerospace manufacturer.

The Washington DC Metropolitan Police Department notified Karras that a teletype request had been received from Hannibal police.

223 KAB69 1510 May 11, 67
METROPOLITAN POLICE DEPARTMENT
WASHINGTON, D.C.

REQUEST NATIONAL CAPITOL UNDERGROUND
RESCUE TEAM THIS CITY STOP. BELIEVE THREE
BOYS TRAPPED IN UNDERGROUND MINE. PLEASE
EXPEDITE POLICE DEPARTMENT

HANNIBAL MISSOURI
FJ 310PM CST SZ

After reading the urgent request, Karras alerted his cave team and quickly called a friend at the Pentagon who agreed to provide the Air Force Two aircraft to fly the SSA team and their gear to Quincy, Illinois' Baldwin Field. He then requested Washington DC police respond with a prompt reply:

E-820 FILE 15 PD WASHINGTON DC 11 MAY 1967
...RUSH...TO...PD HANNIBAL MISSOURI
REL REQ NATIONAL CAPITOL UNDERGROUND
RESCUE TEAM
BE ADVISED SAME IS RESPONDING AND WILL
ARRIVE AT APPROX 11:22 PM EDT AT QUINCY
ILLINOIS.=
/S/ SGT GENE R FILLIUS-CCR

Once Christensen and his St. Louis-based cave team arrived in Hannibal, they met with local authorities and several Quincy cavers who had recently formed the Quincy Speleological Society, a chapter of Karras' SSA. Christensen listened carefully as he was told a survey of all Murphy's Cave passages was not yet complete, and thus far the search had netted only footprints and chalk markings left by other search members.

The Hondo cavers donned their white coveralls and helmets and fired up their carbide lights. "We went approximately ten or fifteen feet into Murphy's and discovered other passages going several different ways," Christiansen explained. "It was just a honeycomb of maze passageways pretty much on one level. I realized it would be very easy for a non-caver to get lost in there.

The fact that you can go multiple directions posed some confusion for novices. Most cavers know how to handle that. As you move through an opening you have to turn around to see what it looks like from the other side, so you're taking mental pictures along the way," he said.

The Hondo cavers found many openings so small only boys could crawl through them. Christensen understood the problem. Most of the Murphy's Cave passages were heavily filled with sediment, so cavers were often crawling along the top of accumulated sediment that filled much of the cave passages' actual rocky diameter. In other words, they were usually crawling around in the higher parts of what would be a much taller cave if excavated of all the silt. Consequently, searchers moved through many of the passages on their hands and knees, with an occasional belly squeeze required, agonizingly slow going in this race against time.

A fifteen-year-old caver, the youngest of the nine members of the Quincy caving group to quickly volunteer to aid in the search, was impressed by Hannibal's underground cave network. He warned one St. Louis caver, "These caves are some of the most dangerous I have ever been in." It was a prescient comment from the mouth of a boy not much older than those being sought.

Christensen's ears perked up when he was informed that other searchers had discovered passages that were blocked due to past collapses. The Hondo team feared collapses might have closed off openings to a subterranean room where the boys could be huddled as the chill settled into their bones. Cavers identified damp passage walls and ceilings, due to recent heavy rain, that might increase the likelihood of a weakness in the cave passages. They'd already found several areas of collapse, and it would take days for the Hondo team to explore all of the collapsed areas as they surveyed Murphy's Cave and the roadcut area to the south. Often, debris had to be shoveled into sacks and removed from the cave. It was slow, physical work.

Caver Charles Blumentrett, a University of Missouri student from Kansas City, excavates a breakdown in a Murphy's Cave passage. Photo courtesy Hannibal Courier-Post.

Two firemen stationed at the local fire station at Birch and Union streets a block away reported they had seen the three boys carrying a shovel and flashlight as they headed to Murphy's Cave Wednesday afternoon. Christensen told his men to be watchful for these items and any other evidence as they continued their search. The boys did not likely have any food or water with them, cavers were told.

As Christensen and his team discussed the unfolding search, they discovered that Murphy's Cave had received the heaviest attention, due to the eyewitness testimony known at the time that placed the boys at the Walnut and Birch cave opening late the previous afternoon.

Part of Christensen's team decided to move three blocks south to assess the Highway 79 roadcut area where the boys also had been exploring a cave network exposed by the heavy equipment during the recent grading work.

"We were especially concerned about the highway area where they had been dynamiting in recent days. Those passages were very prone to collapse," Christensen told searchers.

The Hondo grotto cavers dropped into the roadbed caves and found the worrisome conditions Christensen had anticipated. "They looked normal when you entered them, but the walls and ceilings were totally fractured and very subject to collapse because something unnatural—the dynamiting—had been happening," he explained.

Christensen and his fellow cavers gazed in amazement at what was before them. "I felt it was ready to collapse, like a puzzle just sitting there with all the pieces still in place. Some areas had already collapsed because it was so fractured. It required some daring for us to go through some of those passages."

The roadcut site was now the second strong area of focus for searchers. In previous days, Christensen told his team, the road graders from the J.A. Tobin Construction company, based in Kansas City, had scraped open the top of several cave passages during normal grading activities. The workers had parked the graders over most of these openings overnight to try and prevent the curious neighborhood kids from exploring them.

"We went in and checked other openings and found the roadcut area to have fewer passages than Murphy's," Christensen said. "We could walk upright in many areas, and in some spots the ceiling was twice the height of a man, maybe higher." So far, they'd seen no evidence of the lost boys.

Cavers widen a roadbed opening. Photo courtesy Hannibal Courier-Post.

Christensen established a rescue control operations center in Southside Christian Church, adjacent to the roadcut. With so many cavers and volunteers anticipated, the experienced cave rescue expert knew it was important they had a process to assign tasks and track where cavers and other volunteers were located. A sign out sheet was available in the center and radios were provided to search groups. Cavers and other volunteers not assigned a task or who had just returned from an assignment, would take a seat in the church. As cavers were needed, rescue control staff would radio requests, asking for a specific number of searchers to go to a specified location. Volunteer drivers were available to help with transportation needs.

Mary Jo Deney Powell, who had lived near the Hoags for more than two years before moving across town, rushed to the Southside with her husband and boys in tow to try and offer some help Thursday afternoon. Her two sons, Tony and Randy, were friends with Joel and Billy. "They played together, fought together, traded items, and slept out in pup tents together. It was nothing for me to come home from work and find Billy and Joey in my front room watching TV," Powell said. She knew the Hoags were a happy, loving family.

The Powells joined the other onlookers crowding the sidewalks to observe the search drama. Spotting a police officer, she approached him to relate a conversation she'd had with Billy Hoag two days earlier. "On May 9, we drove over to the Southside to collect the rent on our house," Powell explained. "Billy saw us and came running up to the car gabbing a mile a minute."

While Powell's husband went inside to collect the rent from the tenant of their former residence, Mary Jo stayed in the car to listen to Billy's big news. "Billy was telling the boys about the new cave he and Joey had discovered and wanted my boys to go with them the next day and explore it."

Billy's request set off alarm bells, and Mary Jo quickly interrogated him about where this cave was located. "Billy pointed to the base of a hill below Lover's Leap, nearly directly across Highway 79 and Fulton Avenue," she explained. "He said the bulldozer had broken the dirt off the hillside, and there was a big crack in the hill. He and Joey had seen that it opened into a big room and they were going inside the next morning. I told him how dangerous it was, but he was so excited about finding it that he wasn't worried. I told him to make sure he told his mom where it was and even kidded him about being another Mark Twain."

Billy replied, "Yeah, won't that be something?" Billy, not giving up easily, again asked Mary Jo if Tony and Randy could go with them to the new cave and was told no. "It's too dangerous."

"Okay, bye," Billy said, uttering the last words the Powells would ever hear him say.

Powell related this encounter to the police officer, but "He just wasn't interested. I couldn't get anyone to listen to our story that was told to us by Billy. I tried, but no one would listen. I just never got loud enough, I guess," she later lamented.

The Powells visited with Helen Hoag and other family members who were struggling to fight off fatigue as they maintained an agonizing vigil at the search sites, frustrated the boys had not been found. "If only they hadn't disobeyed us," Mrs. Hoag told the Powells. "The boys had been to those caves often, but their daddy and I told them they weren't to go back up there. They had come home all muddy Tuesday night after being up there. But, like all boys, they just liked to investigate," she said, her voice quaking with worry.

A large crowd of onlookers maintained a constant presence at the roadcut during the Hannibal emergency. Photo courtesy Hannibal Courier-Post.

Cavers continued to pour into Hannibal. Jim Mrozlowski from St. Louis arrived Thursday evening, pleased to learn that Karras was enroute to Hannibal. Mrozlowski first met the noted caver in 1965 and had stayed at Karras' Virginia farm several times with other cavers. "Karras was an adventurous guy. I heard he'd spent some time in Costa Rica searching for gold. He was kind of a character, but anyone who got close to him liked him. He was articulate, and people listened to him. He was a good front man for the search, I thought," Mrozlowski said.

Stanley Sides, a third-year medical student at the University of Missouri in Columbia, had been notified by the Missouri Highway Patrol earlier Thursday that cavers were needed. He quickly left the medical center, retrieved his caving gear and headed to Hannibal with fellow cavers from their Chouteau Grotto Caving Club.

Also along was Columbia land surveyor Don Nicholson, twenty-nine, a respected caver and Hannibal native who had participated in a mapping expedition of Murphy's Cave over a period of several years beginning in 1960. Still, nearly a fourth of the cave remained unmapped. Those particular passages were either too small for adult cavers to traverse or filled in with silt and debris from ceiling collapses over the eons. It was often difficult to determine whether a collapse had happened centuries ago or yesterday.

Sides and his caving compatriots arrived about ten p.m. They quickly donned caving clothing and carbide light helmets and began a methodical search of many Murphy's Cave passages. Nicholson had brought the map that he, Don Myers, Jim Clark, Frank Alexander and other cavers had produced years earlier during their authorized forays into the cave. "We each took a section of the map and began searching to minimize duplication of effort. We probably spent about four hours in there initially," Sides explained.

It was an exhausting, energy-draining shift for the seasoned young cavers, sweat-soaked in the cool environment, as they crawled through uneven, debris cluttered passages. The only human clues they discovered were from previous searchers who had trampled silt and scuffed the clay floors of the passages as they moved through and occasional breakdowns that were being explored for any sign of the boys.

"It's very confusing in Murphy's," Nicholson said after he emerged. "It would wear someone out if they got back in there and ended up panicking because they couldn't find their way out or see where they were going. It could really be a mess," he warned, foreshadowing the community's worst fears.

***

Nicholson had spent his childhood in Hannibal, first exploring Murphy's Cave in 1954 as a curious sixteen-year-old. He'd heard stories about a cousin's father, Harold Bryan, who was briefly lost in Murphy's Cave back in the 1930s. Bryan survived, but his ordeal was fuel for the teenage minds of Nicholson and his caving buddies.

They enjoyed hearing the local lore about the subterranean world below their neighborhood. "Some of us who hung together in high school had heard about Murphy's Cave and had an idea where the cave entrance was," Nicholson said.

Nicholson and his caving friends Larry Howell, Bob Cowder, and Galen King were thrilled Murphy's was so close to their homes. "Murphy's was convenient. We didn't have to travel very far," Nicholson noted.

The teens shoveled out an opening behind the white-washed First Church of Christ located on the northwest corner of Walnut and Birch streets. The small church occupied the building that had once been the home of Joe Murphy, whose family had formerly owned the Murphy's Cave land. "There was a retaining wall about four feet high behind the church. Someone pointed us to it, so we started digging down behind the wall until we got into the cave. The first time we spent about four hours exploring," Nicholson explained. Incredibly, no one had stopped the boys from pursuing their adventure.

"Inside, we found a few names on the cave walls. People from past generations had found their way into the cave from time to time. It was a network or maze cave with passages running in several directions off any one passage. It looked similar to Mark Twain and Cameron Caves only the passages were smaller. If a passage was wide enough that you could go straight through, then it was so low that you'd have to crawl. In areas where it was high enough to stand up, it was so narrow that you had to go sideways, except in some intersecting areas where a 'room' might be found," Nicholson reported.

Murphy's Cave is located within the Louisiana Limestone formation, a largely dry geologic zone overlaid by shale that keeps water out of the cave. Nicholson noticed some of the cave's ceiling extended up into the Hannibal formation, comprised of shale, mudstone and siltstone; and in some places the walls were made up more of this geological composition than the more stable, finely grained Louisiana Limestone. "It was right up at the contact zone where the two geological formations met," Nicholson explained.

This was an important observation as this contact zone might be an area more prone to collapse due to excess surface rainfall.

A dark and foreboding maze cave passage in the Murphy's Cave hill. Photo courtesy David Mahon.

Nicholson wasn't particularly worried about this spot, however. "There was no sign of any imminent danger of the ceiling falling in," he reasoned, "because in those particular narrow passages there wasn't enough span in the ceiling to create conditions for a collapse." But he wondered what more the cave might reveal.

Nicholson estimated they had explored three to five acres of the cave, periodically putting an arrow mark on the wall pointing back to the area last traveled. "There were a few other caves around that same hill around the Bear Creek side that we also explored trying to find a connection into Murphy's Cave but never could find one." After this initial exploration of Murphy's Cave, Nicholson and the others placed a fifty-five-gallon drum into the cave entrance and put a padlocked lid on it to keep kids out.

In the late 1950s, Nicholson had worked as a guide at Mark Twain Cave where he met caver Don Myers, a Keokuk, Iowa native who'd also lived in Quincy briefly before moving to Hannibal. "Don lived a block and a half from Murphy's and was really into the sport. I think he pretty much lived and worked just to go caving," Nicholson said. "He was a very dedicated, experienced caver who loved exploring, making maps of caves, producing reports, things like that."

Dwight Weaver was then-editor of *Missouri Speleology,* the Missouri Department of Natural Resources' caving publication. An experienced caver in his own right, Weaver had traveled to Hannibal to help Myers more fully develop his cave mapping skills.

At the time, maps existed for fewer than fifty Missouri caves, these largely the work of University of Chicago geologist Dr. J. Harlen Bretz and his students whose early explorations and research findings motivated Missouri cavers and geologists to organize the Missouri Speleological Survey in 1956 to identify, map, study and preserve Missouri's caves.

Wearing military fatigues, carbide helmets and paratrooper boots, Weaver and Myers made the best of it in an era when there was little available in terms of high tech, synthetic recreational garb for cavers. "We used baby bottles to store plenty of carbide and these were air-tight so we could stay underground twelve to fourteen hours then. We made do with what we came up with for clothing and gear," Weaver explained.

"We were crawling most of the time on clay and old sediment," he recalled. "There was enough humidity so it wasn't dusty. Don showed me some interesting aspects of Murphy's Cave... calcite crystals in the walls, lots of breakdown in one section of the cave. I

74

found it chillier than other Missouri caves, about fifty-two degrees or so. If you sit still at that temperature you get cold pretty quickly."

During their many forays into the cave across the years, Weaver, Nicholson, Myers and other cavers would compile the first map of Murphy's Cave, spending hundreds of hours underground noting bearings and distances to paint a clearer picture of this complex cave network. Their every move required caution and effort as they drafted the map that would be so valuable during the 1967 cave search. Once completed, the highly detailed cave map's forty sections covered an entire wall in Myer's bedroom like a completed jigsaw puzzle. "We had a bit of a laugh wondering how we could ever replicate it," Weaver said. "But we were able to produce a smaller, less detailed version that still provided a good layout of Murphy's."

***

On Thursday morning, May 11, two Missouri Highway Patrol officers visited the outdoor advertising firm where Weaver worked as an artist. The Murphy's Cave map Weaver helped develop over the years was urgently needed. He turned over a copy of the map to the officers, distressed he would be unable to participate in the Hannibal search. This was a busy season at the outdoor advertising firm with everyone working fifty to sixty-hour weeks, and Weaver's boss had laid down the law, "If you leave, you're out of a job."

The map developed by Myers, Weaver, and others revealed the Murphy's Cave area within the Birch Street bluff included more than two miles of passages in a ten-acre area. The map covered a zone 650 feet by 500 feet, tightly packed with passageways, some walkable, others accessible only by a child due to their small diameters. No one was entirely certain how much more cave existed beyond the mapped zone. "I've explored and mapped at least two miles, and I would say there may be another mile of tunnels not yet explored or mapped," Myers told a *Quincy Herald-Whig* reporter.

Even for this seasoned caver, Murphy's had been a real challenge. "The first time I went in it I was lost five and a half hours before I found my way out. It's not hard to get lost in there," Myers admitted. He also had been briefly trapped in the cave after becoming wedged in tight squeezes that required some digging to free himself.

Myers acknowledged there are plenty of places the boys might be in Murphy's. "Some of those tunnels just come to a dead end. Some are blocked by big solid rocks. I'm afraid the blasting might have loosened the shale and caused a breakdown, crushing the boys or trapping them. It's in the low fifties in there, so it's doubtful they could stay alive long," he said.

Neighborhood ladies outside Murphy's Cave, await any good news.
Photo courtesy Dan Bledsoe.

Meanwhile, the cave teams that had been heavily focused on Murphy's Cave all day Thursday were increasingly skeptical that the Hoag and Dowell boys were in this area of the Southside's underground labyrinth. Still, they brought in heavy equipment and opened up two additional entrances into the hillside to ease a bottleneck and facilitate access into other areas of the cave where collapses had slowed search progress.

Karras and his Speleological Society of America cave rescue team landed at Quincy's Baldwin Field Airport at ten p.m. and were escorted by a state police convoy, arriving at the Murphy's Cave site before 11:30 p.m. The Hondo team members met with Karras late Thursday night, and a review of the facts concluded that no other locations had been thoroughly checked beyond the initial forays into

Murphy's and the newly discovered roadcut cave network.

While Karras gathered his SSA cavers in the shadows of the harsh emergency lights, more representatives of the news media were showing up. Typically, cavers shun publicity, seeing themselves as environmentalists, protective stewards of these natural karst environments. Any distraction they felt only took focus away from the urgent search operation underway. Karras, motivated to garner more attention for his new cave rescue organization, organized the previous fall, and recognizing the importance of the media in keeping the community informed, was all too accommodating of the media's needs. But this publicity-seeking side of Karras' personality was already fueling growing tensions among the other cavers.

Bill Karras, left, with Helen and Mike Hoag during the tense crisis. Photo courtesy Hannibal Courier-Post.

In the wee hours of Friday morning, Stan Sides and his Columbia caving friends emerged from Murphy's Cave into another surreal environment. The unceasing din of power generators cut through the silence of this normally pastoral neighborhood, as bright search lights transformed the zone into a stark landscape of monochrome and shadow. The Columbia cavers were deeply troubled by what they described as a bizarre "carnival-like atmosphere" at the search site.

"Rather than Karras and Christensen working on trying to put together any semblance of an organized attempt at finding the boys, they were romancing the news media," Sides complained.

Karras and members of his team, he said, were roped up, repelling down the bluff for the cameraman from KSDK-TV, the NBC affiliate in St. Louis. "So rather than doing something serious and talking to those of us who had just been in the cave, they were acting like 'rescue cowboys' from out of town with their nice white coveralls and colorful patches, performing for the media and distracting from the search," Sides explained.

It was a devastating critique of the SSA team. Cavers found the media presence distracting as they tried to maintain focus on the formidable task before them. They were also protective of the cave itself. From the cavers' viewpoint, the fewer people that know about a cave, the better it is for the cave and its delicate environment developed over millions of years. And reporters largely unfamiliar with caving often write inaccurate stories, they complained.

Caver Don Myers, who had conducted much of the map charting while the Columbia group was in the cave, estimated they explored about 70 percent of the mapped maze until they ran into marked portions already searched by other teams.

Myers, Sides and Nicholson had little hope the trio was in Murphy's Cave. Nicholson, tired and mud-caked, shared grim news with a local reporter. "I don't think they are in the cave, but the possibility can't be overlooked, so we'll continue looking." Nicholson explained that he still felt confident the boys would be found alive, acknowledging, "It would be, however, a slim chance for anyone to come out without having lights with them."

Around the Murphy's Cave hillside along Bear Creek, in an area long ago called Ide's Hill, there were two other caves. Ure's Cave is located about four hundred yards west of the Murphy's Cave entrances in the back of the hill. Another target, closer to Murphy's

Cave, was Sixth Street Cave. Nicholson, Myers and many others had explored both caves in the past, but this time there was a fresh urgency. Sixth Street Cave, nearest Murphy's Cave, offered less than two hundred feet of passages, and some interesting speleothems— calcite nuggets in the walls and a flowstone created by moisture over the eons. The men accessed the entrance about thirty feet up the bluff within a stone's throw of Bear Creek. The main passage, which varies in height from ten feet near the bluff entrance to 2.5 feet further along the route, took the cavers toward the Murphy's Cave area to the east before they confronted passages filled with silt and other debris. Near the end of the accessible route, another passage made a dogleg right, offering some tighter squeezes as it meandered south and west. The cavers found no sign of the boys in either cave.

The entrance to 6th Street Cave, on the north side of Ide's Hill near the Murphy's Cave entrances on the east side. Photo by Annya Wingate.

After conversations with the lost boys' parents and others in the neighborhood, Sides posited another theory. The medical student suspected that since the boys had been seen carrying a military-type shovel, and cavers had thus far found no evidence of digging inside the cave, perhaps the trio had gone elsewhere on the wooded hillside and dug their own tunnel into the damp earth. "It had been raining for several days, so we theorized that maybe the boys had been digging a shelter or foxhole into the clay hillside, and due to the moisture in the ground, the tunnel had collapsed on them. So we felt we had to start looking for that kind of evidence, too."

A narrow maze passage in 6th Street Cave. Photo courtesy David Mahon

The very scenario suggested by Sides had happened in nearby Quincy, Illinois eighty-two years earlier. On September 4, 1885, three boys, Eddy Klusmeyer, twelve, Charlie Klusmeyer, seven, and eleven-year-old Charles Kaltenbach, were happily digging a tunnel

80

into a sandy hillside on the bluff between Delaware and Washington streets when their fate was sealed.

Once the boys didn't return home they were reported missing, and the parents made every effort to find their sons by placing advertisements in newspapers and offering rewards. Soon, reports came in from people across the country claiming to have seen the boys. One report placed the trio in Keokuk, Iowa where they had supposedly taken a boat. The parents received hundreds of letters from people claiming that the missing boys had been located. Yet every clue resulted in disappointment.

On April 20 of the following year, a man was taking sand from the hillside, when his shovel struck something solid, a human skull. He placed his shovel in another spot on the hillside, and dug up clothing. The coroner was called, and the men soon unearthed three skeletons. Mr. C. H. Klusmeyer arrived and identified the hat, clothes and shoes on the bodies as those of his two missing sons, and the third set of remains was identified as the Kaltenbach boy.

The coroner theorized the three boys had been digging a cave in the hillside when the unstable walls of sand collapsed and buried them so deeply escape was impossible. The three boys quickly suffocated and lay in their self-dug grave for seven months before being discovered.

***

Sides grew increasingly frustrated that Karras would not entertain another theory. "Nobody would listen to us. All the emotion was directed toward a Tom Sawyer and Becky Thatcher style cave adventure." Yes, the boys had explored a Hannibal cave like Mark Twain's fictional characters Tom and Becky, but these boys hadn't yet come home alive.

With the help of Hannibal Police Department Captain Charles Webster, a group of rescuers planned to initiate a surface search of the area as well as a house to house canvass, to pursue Side's theory.

Since the initial police call Wednesday evening, Hannibal Police had treated the unfolding emergency as a missing persons case. Detective Webster, who first joined the police force in 1953, had witnessed the best and worst of humanity during his service, including seven Hannibal murders committed and solved in a single year. But this cave search was like nothing he'd ever experienced. "We handled it as three missing persons, but we found no evidence whatsoever that the boys had run away or been abducted. Given their ages, I don't believe they ran away."

Reverend Elba Martin, the pastor of Lindell Avenue Christian Church, and the former pastor at Southside Christian Church, agreed with Webster. He knew Craig Dowell well and felt confident the boy would never run away or go into hiding. "He was due at home at six p.m. Wednesday to attend a church youth function. I was to pick him up and take him there," Martin told a reporter. "As far as I can remember, he had never missed another church function. It is inconceivable to me that Craig would deliberately miss this one."

"We checked every lead," Captain Webster explained, "and once Karras and his crew arrived in town, the whole situation was turned over to the cave experts." Webster's role then focused on guarding the cave entrances to maintain public safety and control access into the subterranean passages. "There were lots of onlookers, and many were always pressing in close to the action. I just had to make sure only the authorized searchers went into the caves," Webster said.

Detective Webster's wife, Elsie, joined the growing crowd of onlookers, anxious for any good news about the boys' whereabouts. A few years earlier, the Dowell family had lived on Hope Street near the Webster family. "Helen was a sweet lady and a good mother," Elsie recalled. "And Craig was a sweet little tyke who played with our son. During the summer, I'd make pancakes for them every day. They just loved pancakes. At night, they'd play hide and seek with the other neighborhood kids. They were good kids." Elsie didn't believe Craig was the type to take unusual risks, but she knew he was a curious boy. "It's sad," she said. "A cold chill goes through me when I think about it."

By now, a substantial crowd maintained a presence along Birch Street, watching the drama unfold. Groups of concerned neighbors stood with the Hoag and Dowell parents, encouraging and reassuring them. One Southside mother captured the angst that gripped the entire town. "I just stared at the ground. *Where are these boys?* I remember thinking. Were they right beneath my feet? We were so anxious and helpless… the waiting was awful. I just felt like dropping to my knees and clawing the ground with my fingers."

Lynne Strube, fourteen, who lived near the Hoags, remained at the scene for long hours watching the search unfold. Strube told a reporter that, knowing the three lost boys, if they were in the cave they'd be frightened but probably not panicky. He noted that some of the other kids in the neighborhood were taking the disappearance "pretty hard" but doubted the incident would dampen their enthusiasm for exploring. Strube admitted that he would go back into the cave again, but would take a ball of string so he could find his way back out.

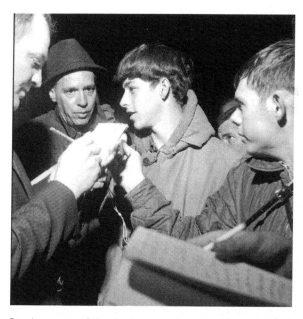

Lynn Strube, one of the last people to see the missing boys, is interviewed by reporters. Photo courtesy Hannibal Courier-Post

A neighbor lady who lived down the street expressed shock as the gossip mill whispered the chilling fact that the Murphy's Cave entrance had been exposed and accessible by curious children for several days.

"Just about anybody and everybody was at the scene, and everybody wanted to help," Conway Christensen said. "There were a lot of non-cavers on scene, so we decided to use some of those people to also help with the ground search. We organized them into groups and explained where to look and what to look for. They were happy to help."

Missouri Governor Warren Hearnes ordered a 150-man National Guard detachment to join the surface search for the boys. They would soon begin a massive, several square-mile search of the Southside's hilly terrain. The plan called for the guardsmen and civilian volunteers to check abandoned shacks, sheds, barns, rail cars, and the river, while also looking for any other cave entrances. Even the Southside's sewer system would be thoroughly checked.

Search personnel already were being pushed to their limits. Caver Jim Mroczkowski, eighteen, a St. Louis native at the time, became ill Friday morning from exposure and fatigue. He'd been pushing himself, desperately searching for more than twenty-four hours straight until he hit a physiological wall. He was taken to Levering Hospital for treatment and kept for observation.

Mroczkowski wanted to immediately return to the search area, but Karras ordered that he remain at Levering until fully recovered.

Knowing time was running out, Karras' team continued to call other cavers throughout the region, requesting their assistance. They needed fresh, well-rested cavers to spell the others already on site. Soon, dozens of additional cavers traveled to Hannibal to join the search, each volunteering for hours to many days.

***

Thirty-year-old Jim Arrigo, a St. Louis machinist, had received an urgent telephone call Thursday as search personnel cast a wide net for experienced cavers. He went home, loaded his car with caving gear and kissed his wife and two children goodbye. Arrigo left Wentzville and headed north on Highway 61, destination Hannibal just over an hour away. The speedometer hit ninety as Arrigo kept a heavy foot on the gas to make good time. Soon, the flashing red light in the rear-view mirror indicated a change of plans. "A state patrolman pulled me over and said, 'Where the hell are you going so fast?' I told him I was going up to the cave rescue in Hannibal. He looked in the back and saw all my gear and said, 'Follow me!' And then I could hardly keep up with him. He was going about 110 when we passed Bowling Green."

Arrigo had started caving in 1959 when he joined the Middle Mississippi Valley Grotto in St. Louis. "I was a city boy, and I liked to go out to the country whenever we could. We explored caves and the wooded areas along the Mississippi River. Once we were old enough to drive, we went out to Meramac State Park and explored those caves." But Arrigo had never been involved in a cave search and rescue operation before, so this was going to be new territory. Once in Hannibal, Arrigo met with Karras at the church headquarters and was immediately dispatched to the roadcut where he was partnered with fellow MMV caver Ann Schallert. In the coming days, the two would spend many hours underground searching for the lost boys.

"There were a lot of people doing a lot of different things, surface surveys, mapping of the cave passages, searching the nearby woods, serving food," Arrigo said. He and Schallert went below into the cave system and slowly made their way through some tight passages lined with horizontal, rough, limestone ridges or ledges common in maze caves. "The passages were laid out like city streets, and so many were rubble filled it would be impossible to dig them all out. You'd travel one hundred feet and there'd be a cross passage. You'd go another one hundred or two hundred feet and there'd be another one. Just like city blocks. Some of the roadcut passages went on for hundreds of feet. But I didn't see anything as large as the passages in Mark Twain Cave," explained Arrigo.

So much dynamiting had been done in previous days that the geology now posed a clear hazard to search personnel, as Christenson had warned earlier. But cavers faced the challenge. "Wherever dynamiting had gone on, it was extremely dangerous. You couldn't get a cop or fireman off the street with no caving experience to do it. We had the know-how to do what needed to be done, so we had to handle it," Arrigo said.

The two cavers made their way down a narrow passage that led from beneath the roadbed east toward the Lover's Leap hill. They found whitish calcite speleothems often called "popcorn" by cavers. "The passage was only about a foot wide with popcorn on the walls, and we were tearing our clothing as we tried to get through that tight spot," Arrigo added. "We were heading beneath the roadcut slope and saw rubble ahead, so we called out to the boys. We wondered what we'd do if we got back there and saw an arm sticking out of the rubble. The thought messed with our heads. We figured we'd tear ourselves up trying to get out of the tight confines. We didn't hear or see anything, so we decided there wasn't anyone back there."

Jim and Ann slowly backed out, releasing fabric from their clothing when it caught on the wall's jagged limestone ridges. They went to the surface, reported what they'd found, and another team promised to check the surface to see if there was a way to dig down to get in beyond the debris they had encountered.

Arrigo spent twelve hours a day underground; it was exhausting and dangerous work. "We'd 'push' the passages as far as we could before we hit debris and silt, then try to find a way around, looking into every nook and cranny. We were always hollering out because the boys could have gone into passages that were too small for adults. We thought they might be hiding or hurt in some corner somewhere."

Karras' instincts were shared with the new arrivals. "Something is holding them in. They are somewhere where they can't get out. Unfortunately, we don't know where that is, so let's find them."

***

Late at night, search leader Bill Karras gets an update from a caver.
Photo courtesy Hannibal Courier-Post.

Nineteen-year-old Hondo member Brian Borton was a late arrival due to work responsibilities. He immediately went to Rescue Control to check-in. "I grabbed a cup of coffee and waited for an assignment," he said.

Observing the action around him, Borton sensed the desperation and tension. "It was a delicate situation, and everyone was trying to maintain composure in a tragic situation." Borton and another caver, Jim Harvey, were quickly called and tasked to search several mines at the cement plant property south of the roadcut zone. A local man gave them a ride to the location.

Borton's interest in caving first emerged during his Boy Scout activities in 1960. He liked the exciting aspect of underground exploration. Later, he met Hondo team members who were operating a member-recruitment booth at a St. Louis sports show. "They were willing to put up with teenagers, so I joined. Conway Christensen lived in Kirkwood and had CB radios, four-wheel-drive vehicles with winches, and lots of other cool equipment," Borton said. "We'd gather weekly for training and practice vertical rope techniques. Conway had been very involved in caving and cave rescue during his days living in Texas. He was a decent guy and a good organizer. We had lots of opportunities to explore many caves."

Borton and Harvey carefully searched half a dozen abandoned mines near Hannibal but found nothing. In the coming days, they would be assigned to search along the river and in nearby forested areas. "We climbed, walked, and searched day and night."

Borton's first trip underground at the roadcut was an introduction to confusion. "It was so disorienting. I crawled through a passage and ended up back where I had started. You had to really pay attention to be confident you'd searched all of your area."

Helen and Mike Hoag maintained a steady vigil at the search locations.
Photo courtesy Quincy Herald-Whig.

Caver Joe Walsh was living in Jerseyville, Illinois and attending Southern Illinois University when he was called by a member of Karras' team. A graduate student in chemistry, Walsh served as the chair of the Little Egypt Grotto, a local cave exploration club. "There was a tremendous amount of excitement and interest among the cavers about the Hannibal search, and my phone was ringing off the hook."

On the five-hour drive to Hannibal, Walsh listened to occasional radio reports about the search as he pondered the unfolding crisis, not knowing what to expect on his first cave rescue mission. "I'd only been involved in active caving for a year at that point, and my interests were more scientific rather than rescue-oriented, but they needed help and it was becoming the biggest cave search in US history. I didn't want to miss out so I went up there."

At Hannibal, Walsh immediately reported to the Highway 79 roadcut site where cavers had exposed three new cave openings. "Two of the openings required rope to reach them because they were higher up, and another was a walk-in opening at the bottom of the bluff. Everybody and their brother were going in and out of there, so I did too."

Walsh initially explored a passage less than one hundred feet in length. "It was maybe three feet wide by three or four feet high, maybe up to six feet high in places." He recognized the geology as tan Louisiana Limestone, occasionally pocked with calcite crystals that would glitter in his artificial light. He kicked at the damp clay floor. "These were not large caves, rather tight and small, the kind of cave you don't really have a good feeling about being in. I did some walking, some crawling, and some squeezing to get through. There were no side branches on this particular one, just a straight shot that went deep into the hill. Soon after beginning to explore the passage, I knew there was no chance the boys were in there."

The consensus of the other cavers was that the boys weren't likely in the other two high passages either because those openings required rope access and had been exposed after the boys went missing. Still, they checked those openings, taking nothing for granted.

Once he exited the cave, Walsh drank in the surrounding environment. The crowd was growing, fed by word of mouth and ever-increasing news coverage throughout the region and beyond. "It was kind of a mob scene. There didn't seem to be a lot of organization. Everybody was just doing their own thing with no direction or guidance from anyone where I was located. I couldn't find anyone to question and people just kept going in and out as they pleased and milling about. I found it to be very disorganized and chaotic. I was warned not to lay my equipment down because someone would steal it and go in one of the caves, and that did happen to other cavers."

Walsh finally sighted Bill Karras in a swirl of blowing dust and ran over to talk with him. "He seemed very pressed and impatient, but directed me to join a team about to search nearby Cameron Cave. I thought that was a wild goose chase because Cameron was gated."

Still, Walsh and several other volunteers dutifully obtained the key from owner Archie Cameron and launched a search of Cameron Cave. "One of my teammates was a reporter, another a policeman, one said he was a firefighter, but the rest were local residents wanting to help." Walsh and the other experienced cavers taught the less experienced spelunkers how to explore by observation. "A lot of people carry string with them, and some make chalk marks along the way, but we go strictly by observation," Walsh explained to them. "You look at the way the rock tilts or dips. You memorize the cave as you go in, note any features or formations you encounter, note the air circulation if any, then you put all this through your mind and eventually get back out of there." Walsh's group spent several hours searching the miles of passages in Cameron Cave and found nothing. After spending a very long day in Hannibal searching, Walsh headed home to resume his studies at SIU in Carbondale.

By now, the army of spectators had overwhelmed the capacity of local police to maintain order and public safety. Director of Civil Defense Bill Broaddus ordered several members of the Civil Defense Police to help Hannibal police maintain order and keep spectators away from unsafe areas.

Local search personnel and teams of experienced cavers from the region had been working around the clock since Wednesday night squirming through the narrow cave passages, and still no trace of the boys.

Cave teams had covered the identified branches of Murphy's Cave, but there was so much more beyond as the passages stretched beneath the countryside. Cords were placed in many passages in the hope the boys could follow one out of the cave if, indeed, they were lost in Murphy's.

After long arduous shifts crawling in cramped cave passages, the dedicated cavers would emerge to debrief Karras and head to the church to wolf down water, coffee and a quick meal. When possible, they'd sink to the ground or slump in a church pew to catch a quick nap before again returning to the subterranean zone.

Karras listens to a radio report from cavers exploring an area south of the roadcut. Photo courtesy Quincy Herald Whig

Karras, the seasoned caver, possessing equal parts impatient showman and steely determination, grew frustrated. "This will make it four times we've been through this cave, and that should convince everyone they're not in here," Karras told a reporter. But, the search team had no other solid leads, so they persevered and kept looking underground, pushing into areas that were passable and digging out newly discovered areas of collapse, a slow, difficult task in the cramped underground passageways.

Hannibal was now ground zero for the nation's caving community. New cavers were spilling into town daily to help with the search and spell exhausted colleagues. Susan DeVier, twenty-three, arrived Friday evening. She had packed her gear and driven to Hannibal after the school day ended at Columbia's Hickman High School, where she taught psychology. A member of the Choteau Grotto, DeVier had grown interested in caving during her senior year in high school. "I joined the grotto out of curiosity and fell in love with caving," she explained. "I loved the social interaction, the people, the camping, being out in nature. And I never minded crawling into tight, muddy spots."

During the ninety-three-mile drive to Hannibal, DeVier and a friend discussed what they'd gleaned from the news about the cave search. "We felt that it was probably a case where three rambunctious boys went off and did something dumb and would quickly be found or wander home."

DeVier already recognized this operation was quite different from other search and rescues. Typically, cavers have a general idea where the missing or trapped persons are located. If they're trapped or injured, rescuers ensure they are kept warm, dry, fed and hydrated until they can be safely extricated by any number of technical means. In Hannibal, cavers didn't really know where to begin. They knew the boys could be anywhere, their conditions unknown.

Once in Hannibal, DeVier quickly stood out among the other cavers, not only because she was one of the few women cavers present, but because standing five foot two and weighing ninety-eight pounds, her petite stature was suddenly a huge asset enabling the search to be extended to many smaller cave passages that the men could not explore. "When I got on scene, someone looked at me and shouted, 'You! In there,' as he pointed a finger at a small roadbed entrance into the cave system. There was a real sense of urgency."

Caver Susan DeVier. Photo courtesy Susan DeVier-Baker

Susan came prepared to go to work immediately. She dressed in a one-piece coverall that offered good protection and wouldn't ride up exposing her skin to the damp, chilly cave floor. For footwear, she wore mesh jungle boots that drained well when wet. She dug into the gear bag and hauled out her helmet and attached the carbide lamp.

She filled her helmet lamp with calcium carbide and added some water into the small reservoir. Once the acetylene gas, produced by the chemical reaction, was ignited, the lamp began to give off a bright white light to break the consuming darkness below. Susan always carried spare carbide pellets in a water-tight plastic baby bottle. "I could get a couple of refills in a bottle that would enable me to continuously search for ten hours or so," she explained.

Susan secured her helmet and crawled down into a narrow roadcut opening, wriggling along with her arms extended ahead of her. "At one point I was under a street for quite a while, and water from a leaking water line was raining down, soaking me."

It was a tight squeeze in spots, requiring her to exhale deeply to reduce her petite torso's girth by a few millimeters so she could make it through the passage. Susan periodically held her hands by her helmet to warm them with the heat radiating from the carbide lamp.

"I carefully looked around, but it was obviously not a productive area, so I slowly wiggled back out."

Hour after hour Devier and the other cavers explored new passageways, conferring with each other, reviewing the early, hand-drawn partial map of Murphy's Cave and resuming their work. "We started early in the morning and went until well after dark, when other cavers would spell us. It was slow, methodical work. We couldn't relax and take a day off. We were either searching, eating quick meals or grabbing sleep when we could," Susan explained. "It was a long, grueling, ungodly schedule. We were so tired and exhausted. All day, all night, slogging away after dark. We just couldn't let up—we had to find them. At one point I fell asleep standing up while leaning against a wall."

Susan DeVier would spend seven days in Hannibal, much of that time underground, assisting with other searches of the surrounding area. "We walked railroad tracks and helped check abandoned factories, sheds and old barns. But most of the time I was underground. We were driven because we knew the boys, if they were still alive underground, were running out of time."

Karras was unusually direct Friday when he told cavers and family members that if the boys were trapped in a small, cramped passageway, with little or no ability to move, they would be unable to maintain their body temperature in the chilly cave environment. When the boys' body temperatures dropped to eighty-six degrees, Karras told them, they would go unconscious; another three degrees would be fatal.

Karras, the SSA leader desiring to raise the national profile on the importance of cave search and rescue services, was feeling the pressure. He'd never led a cave operation where the lost or trapped parties had not been found. In fact, there had never been a US caving case in modern history where the lost person or persons remained lost. Hannibal was on the cusp of making caving history and Karras was at the helm of this worsening human emergency. Privately, he must have wondered if Hannibal would prove to be his worst moment as the nation watched.

Mike Hoag in foreground observes the roadcut search scene. In the distance is the Murphy's Cave location. Kansas City Star photo courtesy of Steve Chou collection.

Chapter 5

"They're below us. Why don't they dig here?"

Quincyan Al Viar and his caving group searched another cave west of the Murphy's Cave hill Friday. The cave, once called Ure's Cave, had been discovered in 1862 and named for a workman who stumbled upon it while digging fire clay to be used for brick production at the nearby brick works. Viar and the others dropped down into the accessible opening in the ground near Bear Creek. But, as other cavers who had come before, Viar's group found only another portion of a maze cave that, they surmised, had long ago become closed off from Murphy's Cave due to collapses and silting.

Viar and the other Quincyans moved to the roadcut where they learned the construction workers' big scrapers recently had opened five holes in the roadbed.

"They had been using explosives and we saw dynamite in some of the passages. Caver Carl Jacobson, who had been an explosives expert in the military, helped to remove and secure some of the dynamite," Viar said.

Viar found that the roadbed cave system was substantial in size. "Passages were everywhere beneath the Lover's Leap hill, well east of the roadbed itself. It was slow going as we explored each one of them. It was a lot like Murphy's, many complex passages only wider and higher."

"We found one passage blocked by a great big ceiling block that had previously collapsed. We didn't dynamite that because we felt it was unlikely the boys would be in the passage on the other side."

With so much focus placed on the roadbed caves, Viar decided to explore higher on the roadcut itself. Walking up the hillside from Fulton Avenue, he traversed the east side of the roadcut when he discovered an interesting new development.

"I looked along this clay hillside, which was about forty feet above the roadbed, and discovered someone had been digging five or six tunnels horizontally into the hill. I entered them on my hands and feet and crawled several feet." Viar said the tunnels were clearly "human dug," with a trowel or small shovel. What confused Viar was the lack of clay debris from the dug tunnels. "No clay piles in sight, anywhere." What had the human excavators done with the clay soil they removed?

Viar carefully moved along the hillside scanning the ground but found no evidence of any other tunnels that may have collapsed. It was a curious find that fed Stan Sides' theory that the boys possibly had been doing their own cave digging when a collapse buried them.

Viar reported his findings to Rescue Control and was tasked with exploring another cave. "Ten or twelve blocks south of the roadcut area, we found a cave that had been revealed when heavy equipment scraped the hillside. It was twenty feet off the roadbed, a ways up." The opening was ten feet by twenty feet, and had been opened length-wise in the Burlington Limestone layer above the Louisiana Limestone layer. "It was a solution cave, much less intricate than a maze cave." Viar explored twenty feet of the short cave passage and backed out after finding no evidence of the three lost boys.

Back at the roadcut, Viar discovered the search team had a new tool in the arsenal. An out-of-state company had donated an expensive, state-of-the-art underground camera which would give cavers the ability to visualize smaller passageways. But it was soon "folly," according to Viar. "We lost use of the camera when someone tripped on the cable, unplugging it. But they plugged it back in wrong and burned out the camera unit." It was a tough loss for the desperate crew.

Reporters, local authorities, and search volunteers wait outside a large roadcut cave opening for an update from the cavers below. Photo courtesy Quincy Herald-Whig.

***

A few miles south of Hannibal, near Illasco, home to many cement plant workers over the decades, lies the Peter A. Labaume Cave abutting the Mississippi. The main opening is very high up the bluff, due to an ancient upheaval of the geologic stratum.

The large main entrance had been closed decades earlier. The cave, named for a french family who once owned the land, was included in the original land purchases made by the Atlas Portland Cement Company in the early 1900s.

The cave had long ago been the site of heavy quarrying and mining activity. From the top of the hill, limestone was taken for cement production. Beneath the cave, a mine had been created so workers could remove shale. A flood in the 1920s had reportedly sent miners fleeing for their lives and drowned several mules used in the operation, requiring permanent closure of the water-filled mine.

Viar, however, knew there was still a way into Labaume from a crevice in the hillside. "There was a steel cable going down into the cave, but we threw a rock into the opening and heard a splash, so we knew it was water filled." Viar didn't believe the boys could have found the opening. "And if they had found their way inside it explains why they'd remained missing. The water is deep." Viar and his team did not explore Labaume given its remote location and poor access, and there is no written record of the Hannibal cave search that indicates Labaume was searched. "If the boys went into that particular cave, they'll never be found," Viar added darkly.

Caver Don Nicholson, also a member of the search team, echoed Viar's concerns about Labaume Cave. Nicholson had long ago been inside this cave, briefly, and described his own chilling experience. "We moved carefully through a passage and came upon an opening in the cave floor. We looked down into the dark, flooded mine below and knew there had been a collapse of the cave floor. We instantly recognized that was a dangerous cave and got out," Nicholson said.

***

Late Friday afternoon, my father and I piled into the family Buick and headed to Hannibal from Quincy, Illinois. We'd moved to Quincy, seventeen miles upriver, after my father accepted a sales position with Oennings, an office supply firm.

This was prime mushroom hunting time, and the warm spring sun was encouraging the prized morels to push their spongy caps through the rich Mississippi Valley soil. Long-time family friend

John Turner, a local printer, had invited Dad and I to his rural property to search for the earthy, meaty delicacies. We knew we'd have success exploring the south-facing slopes, dappled by the sun and rich in moisture among the rotting elms.

After tucking our pants legs into high boots, we started searching the promising, wooded hillsides for morels. Inevitably, our conversation turned to the search for the three lost boys, and we each brought our own perspective to the moment. The Hoag boys were friends of mine, and I knew time was running out. As an adventurous thirteen-year-old boy, still naive about risk, I found it hard to believe that they could just vanish and still not be found.

Dad and John Turner voiced the universal perspective of parents who dread the nightmarish possibility of something terrible happening to a child. "Bud, what would you do if John, Brad or Sharon went into those caves and got lost?" Turner asked.

Dad shook his head and sighed as he plucked a three-incher from the rich earth and tossed it into his bag. "It's a terrible thing to ponder, that's for sure," Dad said.

"It is," Turner replied. "I think I'd give my boy a good spanking for a week, and then hug him tightly for two."

I quietly listened to two fathers struggling with frustration and angst, lamenting the reality of this nightmare-come-true. As we searched some rotting downfall for morels, my face flushed as I grew anxious and overwhelmed by the desperate hunt for my friends. *It could have been me,* I thought.

Had my family remained in Hannibal, I could have been with the boys exploring the complex matrix of caves under the roadbed. It could have been four missing boys instead of three. *Please God, let them find Joel, Billy and Craig.*

The mushroom hunting that spring, normally a much-anticipated annual adventure with abundant reward, was poignantly bittersweet. As we searched our hunting ground among the elms, oaks, and maples, our thoughts were with three boys believed lost below the hilly northeast Missouri countryside. As the sun hung low in the evening sky, we concluded our search, picked thorny cockleburrs from our pants legs and loaded our sacks of morels into the Buick's trunk.

We bid John good-bye and motored north in the LeSabre along the narrow Saverton river road, the shimmering Mississippi on our right, tall limestone cliffs hugging the road on the left.

Dad pulled over near a cliffside spring we'd discovered during a fishing trip a few summers earlier. Cupping our hands, we drank the cold, pure water filtered for eons by the soil and limestone strata. After the refreshing drink, Dad suggested we stop by the Highway 79 search site to try to get an update on the cave search so we wouldn't have to wait until the ten o'clock news. "Good idea," I said.

Shortly, as we stood on Birch Street, it was evident the search was quickly expanding daily, with more cavers arriving to help find the boys. The Mark Twain Emergency Squad and other rescue workers had excavated more large openings in the Murphy's Cave hillside along the west side of Birch Street, just north of Walnut Street.

The newly excavated openings were mere yards from the original entrance the Owen brothers and their friends had used in 1961 when they were lost in the cave for much of a day.

That area was about three blocks north of the roadcut excavation site. The new entry points permitted the cavers additional access into the vast, confusing labyrinth of Murphy's Cave. One of the new openings enabled cavers to get to the other side of a collapsed area discovered earlier. Two police dogs, "Nemo" handled by Jack Floyd of the Hannibal police department, and "Ricter" handled by a St. Louis Police patrolman, were brought in and both animals went to the collapsed area and began excitedly sniffing and scratching the mound of dirt and rock filling the passageway. Suddenly cavers felt they had a solid lead as they tore into the breakdown with shovels. But hope soon faded as nothing was found.

By now, the lost boys story had gone national, a terrible tragedy unfolding in an historic river town made famous by author Mark Twain who spent much of his childhood here. It seemed every child and adult in this town had read the stories about the cave adventures of Tom Sawyer, Huckleberry Finn and Becky Thatcher.

Twain's early twentieth century literary tales were part of the fabric of the river town and the nation. Reporters wanted to better understand this unique story, so cavers were often tapped to take journalists into a somewhat stable cave passage so they could get a better sense of the cave environment.

Cavers enter a large cave opening at the base of the roadcut hill. Photo courtesy Hannibal Courier Post.

Ann Schallert from the Mid-Mississippi Valley grotto was assigned to host a reporter from the Kansas City Star newspaper. Schallert took the journalist down into a roadcut passage, carefully stepping over rubble until they made their way into a passage that stretched out horizontally into the darkness. The reporter, moving along hunched over, looked around, cutting the inky gloom with his helmet light, scribbling a few observations in his notebook as his light reflected brightly off the page. He then took a final look down the passage and told Schallert he was ready to get back to the surface.

The Associated Press and United Press International wire service reporters had also arrived to chronicle the search. "Three lost boys in Mark Twain's boyhood home is a national story," one reporter said to Karras who nodded agreement. "Let me know what you need, and please just stay in the safe areas. We don't need anyone hurt," Karras told the man.

The din of typewriters could be heard clattering away at the downtown YMCA where an informal newsroom had been arranged. Reporters often hung around the search headquarters at Rescue Control, hungry for any fresh information or leads. Just east of the church, Dad and I watched Ed Bradley, a young CBS correspondent from New York, stand with the Highway 79 roadcut behind him, gaze into the film camera lens and soberly inform the national audience there was, not yet, any good news from Hannibal as this desperate, heroic, race-against-time search continued. He signed off with his signature, "Ed Bradley, CBS News, Hannibal, Missouri."

A wire service story published in the May 12, 1967 *Pittsburg Post-Gazette* newspaper captured the flavor of the early national coverage:

Rescuers Searching Cave for 3 Lost Boys

Hannibal, MO (AP) - Rescuers were trying to decide today whether to drill or blast their way into a cave where three latter day Tom Sawyers are believed trapped by a cave-in.

Brothers Billy, 10, and Joey Hoag, 13, and Craig Dowell, 14, were last seen Wednesday afternoon in the vicinity of a newly opened entrance to Murphy's cave, part of a labyrinth of caves and passages lying under the native city of Mark Twain.

Just two miles to the southeast lies historic Mark Twain Cave, scene of Tom Sawyer and Becky Thatcher's fictional encounter with Indian Joe in Twain's famous novel about a young boy's life in this Mississippi river town.

The cave entrance was exposed by construction crews slicing through the south side of Hannibal to build a highway. There were reports the youngsters were seen near the entrances of two caves uncovered by the construction work.

Bill Bridges, vice commander of the Mark Twain Emergency Squad, said it appeared most likely the boys entered a newly opened section of the cave to the West.

Murphy's Cave is only about 50 percent explored and is little known even to long-time residents.

Pearley Palmer, who lives less than 100 yards from the newly exposed cave entrance, said he has lived there 21 years and didn't know there was a cave under the steep hill across the street.

Donald Nicholson, 29, a consulting engineer from Columbia, MO., searched the cave for three hours today. He emerged mud-caked and said, "I don't think they are in the cave, but the possibility can't be overlooked."

Nicholson and Karl Jacobson of Hannibal explored the cave 12 years ago and prepared a rough map.

Don Myers of Hannibal, who did much of the charting in today's search, said, "We followed the outside area of the cave for about 70 percent of the way until we ran into areas checked by other groups. There were no indications the boys were in there."

If the boys are in the caves, Nicholson said, he feels they will be found alive. "It's just a matter of waiting it out," he added. "It would be a slim chance for anyone to come out without lights."

Crowds of people congregated near the center of rescue operations, but there was no excitement - only an air of apprehension among the spectators and the workers.

Bridges said he planned to ask the construction company building the highway to remove a number of large boulders in front of the cave's entrance to make room for drilling or blasting operations, whichever is decided upon.

Bridges said that no one knows with any certainty that Billy, Joey and Craig are in the cave. "The only thing we definitely know is that the boys were seen going in to this Wednesday evening.

Searchers stretched cords along main passages and the entrance of passages known to be dead ends. "It's all very narrow in there." Bridges added, "There are some passages where you can stand up, but most of it is a crawling situation - and I mean crawl."

The highway construction work has resulted in cave-ins in some of the passages.

Nose for Dark Places

Mr. and Mrs. Mike Hoag of Hannibal, parents of two of the missing boys stood quietly near a huge power shovel that only recently exposed the passage that may have swallowed up their children. Neither would speak much.

Craig Dowell's step-brother, Bill Dean, said Craig, also of Hannibal had a penchant for poking into deep, dark places.

Cavers were now discussing whether to drill or blast their way into passages filled with debris. They were looking for more efficient ways to enable their advance through some of the clogged and closed off cave passages without compromising the integrity of the cave's questionable stability. It was a delicate line to walk as cavers pondered next steps.

Their faces and clothing caked with dust and grit, the cavers felt an indescribable fatigue as their unrelenting mission only grew more urgent. They all had a clock ticking in their minds as the countdown was underway on the boys' survival. With no food or water, day three was a critical deadline if they had any hope of finding the youths and bringing them out alive.

***

"They're below us, why don't they dig here?"

Louise Kohler, the second grade Stowell school teacher who was among the last people to see the three boys alive on Wednesday May 10, was back at the roadcut site Friday night. After supper, she'd driven to pick up her sixty-seven-year-old mother so she could witness the historic search activities, too.

"My mother was psychic all her life, very intuitive," Kohler explained. Louise was curious if her mother would sense anything at the scene. The two women arrived on the Southside and it was clear that the cave search was the big show on that Friday night in America's Hometown. The women walked a block or so after parking the car and stood near a redbud tree in a grassy area between the roadcut and the Southside Christian Church.

"Well, my mother looked down at the ground and quickly said, 'They're below us. Why don't they dig here? They're still alive calling for help, I can feel it. I feel like they're weak, but still alive,'" Kohler recalled.

Louise was shocked, knowing her mother would not be reckless with her comments during such a tense emergency. Petite Louise desperately pushed her way through the chaotic crowd of gawkers to a group of cavers huddled around one of the roadcut openings. Pointing her finger, she suggested they dig by the redbud tree some twenty-five or thirty feet west of their roadcut location. The distracted, exhausted cavers tried to focus in the noisy mayhem to hear what she had to say, but their response was less than what Louise expected. "They boo-hooed me." It was upsetting for the devoted school teacher who loved her students. "To me, those three boys were like my children," she would later tell me.

This development was never reported by the news media. Regardless of what the reader thinks about the legitimacy of psychic phenomenon, one has to wonder if the cavers had dismissed a rare lead. If they did embrace Louise's suggestion and widened the search, there is no record of it. Among the cavers interviewed for this book, none were aware of what Mrs. Kohler's mother had to share. The surface digging activity never reached the grassy area where the redbud tree grew. The underground search may have included the suspect area, but a collapse could have walled off the boys so underground search personnel would be unable to reach them. If the boys were, indeed, where Kohler's mother sensed they were trapped, perhaps access from the churchyard downward would have been the best approach to pursue.

***

Karras meets with cavers outside Murphy's Cave during the tense
search. Photo courtesy Dan Bledsoe

By Friday evening, Karras and the other cavers seemed convinced
the lost boys were not in Murphy's Cave. The search team leadership
gathered in Rescue Control and assessed the situation. After two full
days, and more than two dozen searches by many of the Midwest's
best cavers, no evidence of the three boys had been discovered.
Karras and Christensen decided to now turn their full focus to the
roadcut area.

Karras knew that J. A. Tobin Construction's heavy equipment
had exposed five openings in the roadbed and continued filling in
some of these openings early Wednesday evening after the boys
vanished but before they were reported missing. Karras ordered the
construction crew to again try and retrace its actions to locate and
reopen the exposed cave entrances they had filled.

"Let's assume they jumped in one of these caves not thinking
and a Caterpillar dropped a load of dirt on top of them," Karras
theorized to parent Mike Hoag. Mrs. Helen Hoag, who was intently
listening, closed her eyes and shuddered, "It sounds so terrible."

Despite best efforts, cavers were only able to locate and reopen
four of the five roadbed openings. Karras had a persistent sick
feeling as a grave fear rose up and took root in his gut. Since the

fifth cave opening remained elusive, Karras wondered if the boys had slipped into the fifth hole and become accidentally trapped or buried alive by the busy road crew during efforts to strengthen the unstable roadbed. After all, he reasoned, the lads had last been seen high on the road cut, directly above these openings. Karras told his cavers to redouble efforts to locate the underground passage or passages from that fifth hole, but within hours all of their efforts had proved unsuccessful. Frustrated that the fifth opening remained elusive, Karras ordered the exhausted cavers to recheck areas already searched. It was a hard order to hear; some of the searchers had only gotten six hours of sleep in recent days. The frustration was palpable as success appeared increasingly elusive with each passing hour, but the cavers persevered.

An entire nation of concerned citizens was now following the search and praying for the boys. All eyes were on Hannibal as the bucolic town's crisis fed a growing unease. Everyone understood that time was growing short. Young boys dressed in light clothing could not be expected to survive much longer than three days without water, especially in the perpetual chill of what people feared might become a subterranean tomb.

Widen Search For Boys - Rescuers Now Doubt Three Youths Are Trapped in Cave

By Herb Powell and Howard Hoffmaster
Friday, May 12, 1967
The *Hannibal Courier-Post*

Rescuers gave up hope early this morning that three boys missing since Wednesday afternoon (May 10, 1967) would be found in Murphy's Cave and they widened their search for Joe Hoag, 13, William Hoag, 11, and Craig Dowell, 14.

Working in the glare of flood lights, workmen opened a new entrance into a tunnel blocked by a landslide and after digging out the rubble and finding nothing, a spokesman announced that it was now almost certain that the boys were not in the cave.

The new entrance to the cave was punched through after midnight, 30 feet north of the opening that the boys reportedly used when they began exploring the cave at 4:30 p.m. Wednesday.

Rescuers are speculating that after taking a short exploration trip into the cave, the boys may have left for another cave or wooded area.

Bill Karras, national president of the Speleological Society and chief of the national rescue squad took charge of the rescue operations after arriving in Hannibal with a five-man rescue crew around 11:30 p.m. last night.

The new opening was widened with a backhoe furnished by the McIntyre Construction Company.

Mayor Harry Musgrove requested that the National Guard begin a search this morning from the Universal Atlas Cement Plant at Ilasco north along the river to a point beyond the cave area.

Gov. Warren Hearnes concurred in the request and ordered the National Guard company D to join in the search.

Musgrove reacted in response to a request from the Hoag family, which has been unanimous in feeling that the boys are not in the cave, but perhaps in other caves uncovered by construction work or even perhaps in the several pockets of wood and brush land around the cave area.

The Hoag family—mother, father, five remaining brothers and four sisters—were unwilling to standby while others searched, and they organized their own search party. They covered the hills Thursday night.

At 9 a.m. today, the search for the lads had narrowed down to one very small passage, which one "cave man" explained could not be entered unless by someone "driven by fear or panic."

This passage was explored as far as possible and a digger is to be used to open the outer wall on the north side of the new channel to look into it.

The searchers felt certain, however, that if the boys are found in the narrow grotto, approximately 14 feet from the surface, they would not be found alive. There is no indication that the boys are in the passage.

One rescuer, James Mroczkowski, 18, of St. Louis, became ill this morning from exposure and fatigue and was taken to Levering Hospital. Mroczkowski requested to be returned to the search area within one-half hour of hospitalization, but rescue officials ordered that he be kept at Levering.

Since the Murphy Cave area has been so thoroughly searched by now, rescue workers feel that the brushy area south of the cave might yield some clues, and the group has spread out into that area.

There are still some caves in the area which have not been searched.

Musgrove and State Representative Harold Volkmer were making arrangements this morning for hot meals to be served to the searchers.

Captain Gorton of the Salvation Army thanked all the following firms for their donations of food and drinks to workers at the cave the last two nights: National Food Store, Bluff City Dairy, Pastry Box, White Rose Diner, Pennewell's Oil Co. and the A&P.

During the digging last night some chalk was found, but could not be linked to the missing boys since the Mark Twain Emergency Squad, which initiated rescue operations, had used chalk to mark passageways in the cave-riddled bluff, located in the Birch and Walnut street area on the city's south side.

Rescue workers found sticks of dynamite in the area of the new opening, but Karras reported that they were expended charges and presented no danger.

R.S. Bill Jr., president of the Volunteer Mercy Corps. of Houston, Texas, also arrived this morning to aid in rescue operations. Bill was responsible for the rescue of Theresa Fregia, 2 1/2, of Votaw, Texas, on March 18 after she had been trapped in an 8-inch concrete pipe for 9 1/2 hours.

Groups assisting in the search are the Hondo Grotto Underground Rescue, from St. Louis; the Chouteau Grotto Rescue, from Columbia and hundreds of volunteer workers, some of whom are youths very familiar with the caves and tunnels of the area.

Company D of the Hannibal National Guard, 175th MP Battalion, assisted rescuers in controlling the crowds.

Two police dogs, "Nemo" handled by Jack Floyd of the Hannibal police department, and "Ricter" handled by patrolman William Klaeys of the St. Louis Police, were taken to the cave and both dogs went to the side area and began scratching the mound of dirt and rock. This was the reason the new entrance was made—to get behind the slide area.

Search for the three youths began Wednesday night by the Mark Twain Emergency Squad, under the direction of Commander Bob Harrison and Vice-Commander Bill Bridges.

Operations were taken over yesterday by the Hondo Grotto group from St. Louis, under the control of Brother Marvin, of St. Mary's High School in St. Louis. Brother Marvin and the Hondo Grotto were joined by Karras and his team from Washington, D.C., this morning.

R.S. Bill Jr., of the Volunteer Mercy Corps took no active part in the rescue attempts.

The Hoag brothers and the Dowell boy were last seen by Lynn Strube, 14, of 405 Smith, and John Janes, 13, 1125 Sierra, Wednesday afternoon as the trio entered the cave.

Lynn said the youths were carrying only flashlights and a shovel and had no food.

John accompanied the other boys into the cave for 18 feet, and then returned when the trio turned left at one of the hundreds of tunnels that snake through the hill.

Lynn and John both said the Hoag brothers and the

Dowell youth had been planning an exploratory trip into the cave and that all three were used to cave trips.

Lynn said that many youths in the area have explored the caves for as long as three hours and that he feels certain that if the trio was in the cave they would be frightened, but not panicky.

Lynn added that the boys in the area are taking the disappearance of their three friends "pretty hard" but that he doubted that the cave exploration would cease.

When asked if he planned to keep up the hobby of cave searching, Lynn said he would definitely go in again, only he would take a ball of string to find his way out again.

Other boys have been lost in Murphy's Cave up to seven hours, Lynn reported, but they always manage to find their way back out.

At one time in the rescue attempt, five teams of three men each were inside the cave, mapping out the four miles of tunnels and scouring every crack and room. The cave is only approximately four feet high at the tallest point, which meant that rescuers were forced to crawl around on their hands and knees for hours on end.

In some cases, they had to literally walk on the walls, because the bottoms of some of the tunnels were too small to put their feet. Early yesterday afternoon, many rescuers were saying that it seems highly unlikely that the boys were in the cave.

Joey Hoag is in the words of his family "a scientific nut," who likes to poke into dark corners, climb hills, take long walks—anything that will bring him close to his apparently limitless interests.

Joey's curiosity led him, in company with his 11-year-old brother, Billy, and a playmate, 14-year-old Edwin Craig Dowell, into one of the numerous caves under Hannibal, Mo., Mark Twain's home town, Wednesday.

The trio was last seen entering a new entrance to Murphy's Cave, carved out by a construction crew building a road through the south side of Hannibal.

Joey and Craig Dowell are eighth graders at Hannibal Junior High. They seem to be interested in just about everything.

Billy, in the words of his sister, Lynn, has no particular interest. He just likes to do what Joey does. Joey owns a refractor telescope, with which he makes an informed study of the stars. He knows about astrophysics—he wants to be the first man on the moon. Joey also likes snakes, geology, and he likes caves.

Craig, according to his mother, is crazy about bicycles. And just about everything else. He's also a bit stubborn.

"We've talked to him, talked to him, talked to him, about going into these caves. But he's still a boy," said Mrs. Helen Dowell, a cook at the Becky Thatcher Restaurant.

> Joey and Billy have five brothers and four sisters. Craig has three brothers, ranging in age from nine to 23.

> Billy Hoag also is a bit stubborn. He was punished Tuesday night for going into Murphy's Cave, but he went in again Wednesday.

In Columbia, South Carolina, where he was working as a bellhop at the Townhouse Motor Inn, Fred Hoag, eighteen, a brother of the missing Hoag boys, first learned about the search from a co-worker. "The desk clerk heard about it on the radio and told me, so I quickly called my mother from a pay phone, and she was frantic," Fred recalled.

Fred had moved to Columbia months earlier to join his older brother Mike Jr. who worked as a guard at the local prison. Mike also worked part-time as a special deputy who carried a gun and badge. Mike's lifelong aspiration had never varied—he wanted to be a police officer. Back home he'd often visited the Hannibal Police Department to make connections that might lead to a job as an officer. But a candidate had to be at least five-foot-eight-inches tall and weigh at least 160 pounds to meet the department's physical qualifications. Mike fell short by two inches and twenty pounds.

Fred immediately called Mike, delivered the terrible news, and the two flew to St. Louis that evening. The next morning, the two men planned to visit Murphy's Cave and the roadcut area, ready to help.

KHMO radio in Hannibal was now broadcasting news coverage of the cave search almost around the clock as townspeople were hungry for any tidbit of new information. "It was the first thing we heard in the morning and the last thing we heard at night before turning in. It was intense coverage because everyone was so worried," said a classmate of the lost boys. "It was Hannibal's own version of the twenty-four-hour news cycle."

Cavers gather inside Rescue Control for a late night briefing. Photo courtesy Steve Chou.

Chapter 6

"We have blood here!"

Fred Hoag, then eighteen, shuffled nervously along the Highway 79 roadcut, kicking up dust with the toe of his boot and sending a small rock skittering across the construction site. He was having a hard time masking the frustration he felt. Not a single clue about the boys had been found, and he worried the boys might already by dead.

We have to find them today, he thought.

Karras and Christensen arrived and hustled Fred into the church where he was briefed on the search effort to date. Fred was issued a helmet and carbide light, and the trio made their way back to the roadcut so the distraught brother could join the massive search for Joel, Billy and Craig.

Helen Hoag, wearing a tweed coat to ward off the morning chill, gave Fred a hug and whispered, "Be careful son." In this poignant moment, the grieving, despairing mother of eleven could only focus on a third son now confronting a worrisome, uncertain destiny underground.

It seemed like the air was being sucked out of Hannibal's Southside. Growing tensions, worry and fatigue had morphed into a painful and persistent triad of emotions. Helen and Mike Hoag and Helen Dowell, along with their kids, were in uncharted territory. The prospect of losing children is foreign to a parent's heart and soul. Moms are built to birth and nurture for a lifetime. Dads teach their boys to fish and hunt, to navigate the boundaries of life as they transition from boyhood and grow into self-reliant, responsible men. This was all new; kids should never go before the parents. It was just unnatural. Still, they somehow maintained hope.

Helen Hoag hugs son, Fred, before he enters the roadcut cave network. Photo courtesy Hannibal Courier-Post.

Fred teamed with Conway Christensen for his first cautious foray into the roadcut cave system. He was in awe of the dark labyrinth beneath the neighborhood where he grew up. And being a young man himself, he understood the power these caves must have had on his brothers and Craig. "Any boy would have been fascinated by the cave. It was Tom Sawyer through and through, and I saw why the three boys were all in," Fred recalled.

As Fred emerged from the cave, his father offered a helping hand as he made his way up and over a final pile of debris at the edge of the cave entrance. "The passages were small, but you could get through most of them," he told his family. "It was dry in there and cool. I know the temperature could be a problem for them, along with having no food or water."

Standing on the roadbed, Fred drank from his canteen and took in the scope of this remarkable, herculean search effort. Despite the myriad of emotions he was feeling, he held onto a fleeting glimmer of optimism that enabled him to see the best of this terrible situation. "There was so much faith and support being shown by everyone for our family," Fred noted. "The goodness of man came through. Something good can be found in every disaster, and it was clear to me in that moment that mankind is loving and giving."

During a break from the action, big brother Mike Hoag, Jr. (Mickey) and his sister Lynnie took a walk up Riverside Street near the Hoag homestead. Each sibling became the other's therapist as they poured out their fears, concerns and hopes. "Mickey and I were close," Lynnie explained. "During that walk, he turned to me at one point and said, "'I want you to remember this—if I could die so they could live, I would.'" It was a poignant testimony from the core of his being, evidence that this close family remained tight and supportive despite the terrible trauma rocking their world.

***

Nationally, the massive search was drawing reaction from a relative of Samuel Clemens. Cyril Clemens, the sixty-one-year-old editor of the Mark Twain Journal tried to maintain a sense of optimism despite the troubling lack of evidence in the search. "I know the folks are concerned, but I feel confident the lads will get out without harm," he said to a reporter. "If the three boys are in the cave, I think they'll find a way out. We grownups don't give the youngsters credit for their smartness. I feel the boys will come out okay."

Townspeople held onto this hopeful opinion expressed by a man who'd personally known Laura Hawkins, the real-life Hannibal girl behind the fictional Becky Thatcher character in Twain's writings.

Still, an air of apprehension grew more palpable as the around-the-clock cave search continued. Raw with fatigue, nearly two hundred cavers and other search personnel were now caught up in this race-against-time odyssey. They were spread out from the two main search locations, across Marion County into Ralls County. Searchers even took to the air in light aircraft to scan the river and countryside. McDonnell-Douglas Aircraft in St. Louis sent a military aircraft with high-tech, side-scan radar that produced detailed imagery. These photographs were helpful to ground volunteers searching wooded areas and several islands in the Mississippi River.

As the tumult continued, history had quietly been made. Hannibal had officially become the site of the largest cave search in US history. The scope of the search required Karras to enhance communications among the growing number of search teams. He solicited help from Pete Strode, the president of the local Beacon Light CB Club. Strode contacted Lafayette Electronics in New York for several five-watt Dyna-Com 5 walkie talkies, the only portable transceivers that worked satisfactorily underground, in Karras' opinion. Strode also supplied three base stations and a dozen or more portable CB radios to ensure around-the-clock contact was maintained with all search teams.

Christensen and teams of cavers continued searching scores of additional caves and ground openings that had been reported around the Hannibal area. "It appeared that for every cave we searched, two more would be reported to us," Karras complained. "Caves were everywhere. One could almost say the Hannibal area was just one huge cave-riddled piece of acreage."

Don Myers informed Karras he'd completed mapping as much of Murphy's Cave as possible. He could do no more because the remaining passages were too small and unexplorable by adult cavers. He'd found rescue markings everywhere in the cave indicating the rescue teams had thoroughly, and repeatedly, searched the mapped portions without finding a trace of the boys.

Still, Myers worried that recent construction activity had compromised the cave; he feared the boys might be in a passage now unreachable, perhaps blocked by debris from a recent ceiling collapse. "What worries me is they have bulldozed and blasted through the northeast area of the cave. I warned the highway department at the time that it would cause trouble because kids in the area would be exploring new entrances," Myers explained to a Quincy reporter. "I'm afraid the blasting might have loosened the shale and caused a breakdown, crushing the boys or trapping them. It's doubtful they could stay alive in there long."

Caver Morris Grumbine inside a roadcut passage. Photo courtesy Morris Grumbine family.

Exhausted caver Jim Mrozlowski, who'd been searching since his arrival Wednesday night, was forming his own opinion after spending endless hours in cramped roadcut cave passages, many of them now geologically unstable. "It was pretty cut and dry in my mind at the time," he explained. "They had been dynamiting the area for several days prior to the boys' disappearance. We knew those roadcut caves were fractured. I'd heard blasting caps and dynamite had been found unexploded by a construction worker on the roadcut. Maybe the boys found explosives and tried to use it to widen a passage," he said.

It was another theory, but one with sound footing. Karras claimed hundreds of sticks of dynamite were used during the massive earth-moving project, some of which did not explode. "Several times during the excavation, some of this dynamite was exposed, complete with wires and blasting caps intact," Karras reported. Those explosives were safely defused.

But while digging in a roadbed hole, backhoe operator David McIntyre stopped his rig, threw his hands in the air and yelled, "That's all!" Ahead of his machine lay three sticks of dynamite wedged between rocks, one with the blasting cap and wires still attached. One stick was defused, and the other two sticks were detonated in a safe area, and the search resumed.

Caver Jim Arrigo said search personnel were always finding blasting caps left over from the recent detonation activity prior to the boys' disappearance. "We also found blasting caps that hadn't exploded and were lying around live. We found enough to fill a bucket," he recalled.

***

Three of the best speleologists in Missouri had now arrived in town to join the desperate search. Jerry Vineyard, who worked for the Missouri Geological Survey, would later become a lifelong leader in promoting the identification and stewardship of the state's cave resources. Gregory "Tex" Yokum and Langford "Lang" Brod, both experienced and serious cavers, represented the Middle Mississippi Valley Grotto, which had been established in 1958.

Yokum was considered a great field geologist and was widely respected in caving circles, despite having had no formal geology training. "He was one of the most intelligent men I've met," said Joe Tripodi, a member of the Middle Mississippi Valley Grotto who had joined the caving group in 1962 while still in high school. "Tex could sit down and talk geology with anybody. I learned a tremendous amount from him. Tex also was an excellent cave mapper and cartographer. He drew some beautiful cave maps."

Yokum was considered an expert on the caves of Perry County which has more caves than any other Missouri County. Back in October 1961, when Perry County had only forty-four of its many caves identified, Yokum, Brod, Stan Sides, Dennis Drum, Jack Palmer and Steve Sabo were exploring Tom Moore Cave during a mapping trip when Sides notices a small foot-long breathing hole at the foot of a ground sink.

Sides and Yocum dug out the hole until it was wide enough to slip through and entered another subterranean world. Before them was a virgin cavern so vast their carbide lights could not fully cut through the darkness. The men had discovered what would later be named Berome Moore Cave with more than eighteen miles of mapped passages.

In the following decades, the cavers would be part of the growing speleological wave that identified more than 675 known caves in Perry County, including Missouri's longest, Crevice Cave, with more than thirty miles of surveyed passages.

Lang Brod was another mentor for Tripodi who had now assumed a post in Rescue Control at Southside Christian Church. "Lang was an engineer by training and tended to look at caving from an engineering point of view," Tripodi said. "He observed everything. Lang saw things that nobody else saw. He was a great mapper, too. These were great people to have in Hannibal."

Jerry Vineyard, an avid caver, Missouri's Deputy State Geologist and a graduate of the University of Missouri Columbia, arrived in Hannibal a bit late due to the birth of his daughter days earlier. With his wife and daughter now settled at home, getting plenty of help from family and friends, Vineyard had made a dash to Hannibal to spend four days searching.

Upon arrival, he quietly recognized a transition had taken place, from a search and rescue mindset to a body recovery operation. And, it was a scene unlike any he had ever experienced. "People were running around, and it was pretty much chaos," Vineyard explained. "There were many theories and different folks floating in and out of the picture. It was quite a circus, and quite a media circus."

Vineyard knew Karras and Christensen were very rescue-focused and always willing to assume a high-profile posture to promote their cause when necessary. "They had fancy uniforms and all the equipment and were keen to raise awareness of cave rescue. They made quite a splash. Cave rescue was a big thing for them. That's not a bad thing at all, but these guys were seen by many as publicity seekers and trying to just do things their own way. It rubbed a lot of people the wrong way."

After speaking with Karras and Christensen, Vineyard went below ground to assess the newly discovered cave network. "There were several large passages beneath the roadbed, ending in typical Louisiana Limestone fashion, with surface fills (silting) against the valley occupied by Riverside Street to the west," Vineyard reported with the precise, descriptive language of a geologist. "Other passages led farther into the hill beneath Lover's Leap, interconnecting in a bewildering maze of tight, difficult-to-follow passages." Many other small passages, he noted, led toward the roadbed but were terminated due to their small diameters or roof collapses, likely due to the recent drilling and blasting.

Vineyard recognized that geology was the overriding consideration in this tragedy, and he well understood the enormous task facing cavers. "The nature of the caves is such that becoming lost is an ever-present danger, and the possibilities for access to complex maze caves are endless."

Tripodi, from his position in Rescue Control, had a good sense of the overall effort. His control center included map-covered tables that search leaders used to identify areas of focus across the Hannibal area and nearby Ralls County. Cavers and other volunteers would sign in and out of the log book, report their findings, and get another search assignment. Tripodi believed the search was going as well as could be expected with so many people involved. But, like Vineyard and others, he too sensed Karras was irritating many regional cavers who typically shun publicity, put their heads down and stay highly focused on the mission before them.

"To be perfectly honest with you, Karras was more of a publicity seeker. He was around, but we could have done just as well without him. He was our main media guy, he did the interviews," Tripodi said.

Vineyard and Karras conferred frequently during the search, maintaining a professional relationship. "He'd ask what I thought or where I thought they should concentrate the search. We worked together, but he handled pretty much all the interactions with the press and the local folks," Vineyard explained. "He loved the limelight and was busy running around trying to control everything. It reminded me a lot of the chaos and confusion surrounding the Floyd Collins cave rescue in Kentucky in 1925," Vineyard added.

Floyd Collins was an avid Kentucky caver who became trapped fifty-five feet below the surface, and 150 feet from the entrance, while exploring Sand Cave in January 1925. At the time, he was searching for a new route into Crystal Cave, the show cave he had discovered on his parents' farm in 1917.

Rescue personnel knew precisely where Collins was located, but his foot had become trapped by a falling rock that immobilized his body in a steeply angled and coffin-tight passage.

Despite a fifteen-day effort by hundreds of rescuers, who found themselves surrounded by a sideshow of gawkers hawking maps and moonshine, the trapped Collins slowly slipped away as his body temperature fell and his heart gave a final sluggish beat—death by hypothermia. The Collins incident was one of the biggest stories of the era, a calamity that kept an entire nation on edge as Americans followed daily newspaper accounts of the rescue attempt.

William Burke "Skeet" Miller, a cub reporter for the *Louisville Courier-Journal* newspaper, who due to his small stature actively participated in the rescue by taking food, water, and words of reassurance to Collins, won a Pulitzer Prize for his series of articles on the rescue attempt.

***

Cavers working at large roadcut cave entrance.   Photo courtesy Quincy Herald-Whig.

Forty-two years later in Hannibal, another high-profile rescue now gripped the national psyche, and one of the main characters in this human drama was the geology that birthed these impossibly complex caves.

As a geologist, Vineyard knew hilly Hannibal well. Like icing on a cake, the hills and bluffs were capped with Burlington Limestone, the dominant raw material needed for cement production. A study conducted in 1849 by University of Missouri geology professor George C. Swallow had first identified the presence of abundant deposits of limestone and shale. Below the Burlington layer, geologists found a stratum of Louisiana Limestone, named after the nearby town of Louisiana, Missouri where it was first described, measured, and later named in 1892 by Missouri's twenty-eight-year-old State Geologist Charles Rollin Keyes.

Louisiana Limestone is perfect for maze caves formation. These caves were created when an ancient sea covered the area, water percolating through the limestone and, over time, creating complex, tentacle-like passages. Keyes first observed that the regular natural joints in the Louisiana Limestone often gave the appearance of a man-made masonry wall. While largely dry, thanks to shale layers above and below, maze caves are cooler than most other Missouri caves further south. Vineyard knew anyone immobilized beneath the ground for long would quickly succumb to hypothermia.

In the late 1950s, during his college years, Vineyard worked summers for the Missouri Department of Natural Resources, driving a jeep around Missouri looking for caves and recording information in the state's growing cave database. It was a dream job for the young man whose passion had been fueled by childhood explorations of the caves and springs on his family's farm near Dixon, Missouri.

Vineyard had joined the state geological survey staff in 1963. "And one of the first jobs they handed to me when I walked in the door was custodian of the cave files," Vineyard said. It was the happy start of four decades of cave work for the state agency as Vineyard rose to the position of Deputy State Geologist and earned the respected moniker "Father of Missouri Caving."

During his professional time with the agency, the number of identified caves in Missouri grew from 256 to more than 5,500 by the time Vineyard retired in 1997. "We worked cooperatively with cave groups and property owners to accumulate an enormous amount of information, and we probably have the most extensive files on caves of any state in the country," Vineyard explained.

We have blood here!

Suddenly one of the observers motioned to Yokum. "Tex, I'm afraid we may have a hole full of blood here." Tex watched as the observer moved his foot to reveal a drill hole with a reddish liquid oozing from it. They kept it quiet, not wanting to panic the crowd and create unnecessary excitement for the media. "We took a sample," Mozlowski explained, "and caver Ann Schallert, who worked as a lab technician in St. Louis, took it to a Hannibal hospital for analysis."

The twenty-three-year-old Schallert soon came back with an answer for waiting cavers—the sample was not blood. The cavers conferred with the construction workers and determined the red liquid was from a fertilizer component they had packed into the drilled holes for blasting the roadbed and roadcut prior to the search. The material, they explained, turns red in the presence of water.

Yokum and Vineyard studied their fellow cavers at the roadcut and saw they were exhausted and frustrated by the lack of progress. The boys could be anywhere, and if they started digging until they found the bodies, they might be digging up nearby private property for many days. Going below the roadcut, cavers noticed that if a passage was filled in or collapsed it may not be visible and available for complete searching, so cavers were never fully certain they were exploring the totality of their assigned zone.

Tex Yokum repeatedly sent several teams to different areas of the roadcut system to double-check them. He personally tackled the excavation of a large breakdown pile in a particular cave passage that had been exposed earlier. "Our excavation turned up nothing," Yokum reported.

Caver Ann Schallert wanted a closer look. A member of the Middle Mississippi Valley Grotto (MMV), she had extensive experience caving in southern Missouri, but this was her first time exploring an unmapped maze cave. Schallert had first grown interested in caving while in the Girl Scouts. Now she was part of the largest cave search in US history.

"It was kind of scary," she said, recalling her trips into the roadcut cave network. Dressed in blue jeans and a denim jacket, Ann fired up her carbide lamp and carefully made her way down into a craggy, cave entrance. "There was a lot of breakdown, large slabs of limestone that I had to crawl over into the passage. Most of the slabs were stable and too big to move, but some would tip and move as you traversed them." Schallert found she could walk upright through some of the cave passages, but would have to frequently drop down on all fours and crawl through others. "There were big slabs of rock down and jointed passages going in many directions." She moved slowly, gazing upward and looking for any side passages and then downward carefully, watching her steps as she moved over debris in the cave passages.

Schallert emerged an hour later and agreed with Yokum that a better map of the complex roadcut network was desperately needed. "This cave is extremely complicated and virtually impossible for us to keep track of the areas being examined," Yokum reported to the SSA's Karras.

A group of experienced cavers were each assigned a section of the roadcut cave system to survey and map. Using nylon cord with distances marked every five feet, cavers would extend the cord from a starting point to another point in each passage. They took measurements and used a compass to get the bearings down each of the many passageways. This was slow, methodical work that demanded accuracy.

Schallert and her MMV colleague Joe Tripodi, both cave mapping specialists, began mapping the known surface entrances to better orient surface features with the maze cave below. "We used the surface map to show the relationship of all the underground passages. Some of those passages didn't connect, and we were mapping to tie in everything," Tripodi said.

When he and Schallert later emerged from the roadcut cave system, the caving duo expressed surprise that so many passages could be packed into a relatively small footprint. It was Tripodi's belief that the roadcut cave and Murphy's Cave were artifacts of a much larger karst system that "eroded away a very, very long time ago as the valleys were formed, much as Mark Twain Cave and Cameron Cave are on opposite sides of a valley, but were probably once connected because the caves are older than the valley which was created by drainage and erosion over time."

Soon, bits and pieces of a detailed map came together into a more coherent view of the roadcut system. "With this map, we [can] predict precisely where a passage would be in relation to the roadcut," Yokum reported. The map also ensured cavers assigned a particular area to search actually arrived at the correct underground location.

Caver Earl Barnes discusses the updated roadcut system map with other cavers. Photo courtesy: Hannibal Courier-Post.

Caver Jerry Vineyard combined the mapping results with his personal cave assessments and painted a stark and complex picture of the cave network for search personnel. Vineyard told his fellow cavers the roadcut system likely contained more than a mile of impossibly complex passages. Many of them, he explained, were silted in from surface materials over the eons. "It is possible, even for small boys, to dig through terminal fill to gain access to the cave networks beyond," Vineyard said, meaning the boys might be anywhere in the cave network, and it was possible they could have dug out and traversed silted passages too small for adult cavers.

"The caves are complete mazes," Vineyard further explained, "and it is extremely easy to become lost, for landmarks are few and passages are monotonously similar. Passages are high and narrow, with rough, horizontally ridged walls caused by differential weathering. Ceiling heights usually are much greater than passage widths, but because the widest part of the passages is usually the lowest part, crawling may be necessary when the upper part is too narrow to pass through."

Mapping of the cave showed several large passages below the roadbed and ending against the valley occupied by Riverside Street. Other passages extended farther into the hill beneath Lover's Leap, again interconnecting in a bewildering maze of tight, difficult-to-follow passages, Vineyard reported.

Numerous small passages led toward the roadbed but were terminated either because they became too tight or because of roof collapses when the Louisiana Limestone was drilled and blasted to roadbed grade. The take-away conclusion was clear—the cavers had an incredibly challenging task still ahead, and while searching for the lost boys, they were jeopardizing their own lives.

The new map led to the discovery of an old cave entrance at the end of Swan Street, east of the roadcut bluff. A backhoe operator dug into the asphalt street, exposing the cave entrance about five feet below the surface. The passage appeared to join the roadcut cave network, though it was an extremely tight side passage.

Petite caver Susan DeVier, all ninety-eight pounds of her, was dispatched into the tight passage. She wriggled like a mole through the cramped space, alone with her thoughts and frustrated by the lack of progress being made in this historic search. "I remember the insanity of it, knowing that if the boys were injured, exhausted and suffering from hypothermia, they were likely unable to yell for help." Susan explored the totality of this newly discovered side passage and found nothing.

The boys could be behind or under a collapsed area, but where? she later pondered. There were just too many tight, narrow passages and too many possibilities.

"You might miss them by inches and never know it," Vineyard said.

"And we can't dig up the entire area," Mrozlowski chimed in. "An awful lot of money had already been spent with the construction delay and the growing rescue operation."

Mrozlowski and others said construction workers had seen exposed cave openings quickly fill in with dirt and brittle rock as the heavy equipment lumbered down the roadcut before the boys vanished on May 10. They theorized something bad may have quickly happened to the boys before anyone had even noticed they were missing.

One such hole had suddenly been revealed in the roadcut, and the highway foreman, nicknamed Stoney, indicated it was five feet deep with loose debris falling into it. "We called that opening Stoney's Hole," Mrozlowski said. "Stoney had briefly left the area, and within the span of five minutes that hole had closed up on its own as roadbed debris collapsed into it. Just disappeared."

Mrozlowski now had his own sense about what possibly happened on May 10. "I think the boys jumped into a hole, went into a cave passage and it collapsed or was filled in. The boys had been told to stay out of that area, and using teenage logic you can imagine what they did."

A bold effort was launched to find Stoney's hole. A large D-9 Caterpillar tractor, equipped with a powerful ripper that could tear through rock, was brought in to carefully open up an already-searched portion of the roadbed network. The big Cat began the slow work of opening an area one hundred feet long by twenty feet wide down to the floor of the cave passages.

Two days later, the big Cat was digging along the face of the roadcut when lo and behold Stoney's hole was finally rediscovered. Unfortunately, it provided only false hope as once explored it revealed no evidence of the boys.

With the passages nearest the surface of the roadcut thoroughly searched and now ripped open, it was time for the next phase. "With everything pretty well exhausted, we were removing the debris with a big steam shovel," Christensen reported.

Vineyard climbed aboard the massive Bucyrus-Erie 88-B steam shovel that was carefully quarrying the roadbed. This digging enabled cavers to remove surface material so they could see behind collapsed areas that were unreachable from below ground in the tentacle-like passages.

A big earthmover digs out an already searched area of the roadbed in a last ditch effort to find the lost boys. Photo courtesy: Hannibal Courier-Post.

Standing on the Bucyrus-Erie's walkway, outside the shovel operator's cab, Vineyard kept his eyes on the digging activity as the big shovel repeatedly scooped up tons of limestone and earth with each bite of its five-cubic-yard bucket. "We always kept a man on the shovel to look for any signs of the boys as they dug away the roadbed surface," Vineyard explained. Three large dump trucks hauled the limestone debris up the roadway where it was used as fill in a low spot on a future stretch of Highway 79.

From his vantage point standing on the big shovel, Vineyard could see the Murphy's Cave site three blocks to the north; onlookers lined both sides of Birch Street, as if awaiting some perverse parade.

Joe Tripodi, one of the St. Louis-area cavers, had the tense debris inspection assignment for a few days. "We'd fill trucks with rock and debris and inspect it as it was loaded and unloaded. What we didn't tell anybody is that we were looking for body parts or the boys' shovel and light, some kind of a clue that the kids had been in there. And when we dumped the debris, I'd watch again for clothing, body parts, blood or whatever. But we never found anything."

Onlookers grew alarmed seeing the big ripper tearing up the roadbed and the giant shovel gobbling up earth and rock, but Karras knew it was necessary. "Our maps and physical surveys indicated several areas containing large breakdown piles that could only be examined safely by removing the roof of the cave and going in from the top," Karras explained. "The disappearance of Stoney's Hole was proof enough of the need to examine all suspicious breakdowns."

Still no sign of the boys was found after the extensive quarrying of the roadbed. Frustrated, Karras and Vineyard wiped the dust from their faces and decided to take a rare break for a sandwich and some coffee before resuming their work.

***

Volunteers helped staff Rescue Control at Southside Christian Church.
Photo courtesy Hannibal Courier-Post.

This throng of hard-working searchers required an extraordinary amount of food and drink, so the Hannibal crisis was a moment for the church to shine. The ladies of Southside Christian Church, located just adjacent to the roadcut site, prepared countless meals and recruited additional help from neighborhood residents to help prepare food and serve meals during the search. This important work was supplemented by dedicated helpers from the Salvation Army, local churches and restaurants, and the American Red Cross.

"The city of Hannibal was incredible," caver Tripodi said. "We were so impressed with how they took care of everybody. I've never eaten so well. Every meal was brought in by the local people, and everyone brought their best dish. The food was amazing, and there was always more of it than we could eat. I don't ever recall going to a restaurant to buy a meal."

And the generosity extended beyond free meals. "A local hotel was giving us rooms for free and the cab company was giving us free transportation. The Hannibal people were amazing," Tripodi said.

Ruth Martin Ellison, whose father had previously pastored Southside Christian Church, was back home on college break for several days. The Lincoln Christian College sophomore was awed by the human dedication she witnessed as she served the exhausted cavers and other volunteers at mealtime.

"The searchers were very dirty from crawling around in the caves. I have a vivid memory from serving at one particular mealtime. As I was refilling drinking glasses, I saw one of the men with inch-long, whitish-beige worms crawling in his hair. I realized just how much these men were profoundly dedicated to finding the boys at all costs," Ellison said. "I'm sure they had to wash out worms and bugs from their hair, clothes and bodies every night. They came from all over to help. It was extraordinary."

Ellison spent many hours watching the search drama, pondering the influence Mark Twain's literature had made on Hannibal's impressionable children. "Many of the kids used to go into the caves under the Southside." Ruth explained that the parsonage adjacent to the church was built atop the caves, as were some other homes. "Our living room was always cooler, and you could often smell the cave below."

Ellison and her father, Pastor Elba Martin, drove to the Dowell house on nearby Union Street to see how the family was holding up during the terrible crisis. The Dowell boys often attended Lindell Avenue Christian Church, which had been started by Pastor Martin in 1965. "Mrs. Dowell was devastated," Ellison said, "but she was still hopeful the boys would be found. Craig's older brother Mike wanted to go out and help search. It seemed like it was very hard for him to just sit at home and wait."

After visiting with the Dowells, Ellison thought about the boys' situation, what it would be like to suddenly find yourself trapped, hurt, hungry and scared. "I just can't imagine the horror of knowing you can't get out and would slowly die." She returned to the church to help with the food operation, such an important role to keep the search personnel fueled for their arduous physical duties.

At Jesse Sorrell's modest green house at 323 Fulton Avenue, not far from the roadcut location, the kitchen had become one of several bustling, culinary operations. She and the other ladies in the neighborhood were busily helping feed the search crews around the clock.

On a May morning, Jesse and granddaughter Joyce Sorrell, a friendly and big-hearted Southside native, busily prepared sandwiches, coffee and lemonade. As they wrapped bologna sandwiches in waxed paper, the two talked about the search and how Hannibal's adults were keeping a tighter rein on their kids and grandkids since the boys had gone missing.

Joyce, a classmate with Joel Hoag and Craig Dowell at Hannibal Junior High, had spent fitful days and nights worrying about the boys. "I was devastated," Joyce explained. "I had such a crush on Craig. Oh, what a cutie he was with that long curly hair." She described Craig as a serious boy with a good sense of humor. "He wasn't reckless. He always acted responsibly," she said. "After school we'd often hang out at the Stowell School playground. Craig liked to be the leader when we explored the storm drains on the Southside."

Yes, you read that correctly. Many Hannibal kids had explored the storm sewer during the 1960s. The curb drains had spacious openings to accommodate the large volumes of water coming off of the Southside's hilly streets during downpours.

In dry weather, kids would squeeze through the curb openings and follow the storm sewer until it exited into a rocky creek bed that ran along the backyards of Fulton Avenue and Union Street homes and then moved underground behind the Southside Fire Station at Union and Birch streets. The practice of playing in the storm sewer largely ended when a child was swept away and drowned during intense flash flooding.

Joyce understood why Hannibal's kids loved to explore. After all, they'd read Mark Twain's books and stories, still very much an influence in the lives of twentieth century children. Imaginations were easily stirred by the adventures of Tom Sawyer, Huckleberry Finn and Becky Thatcher.

After delivering sandwiches and beverages to the Southside Christian Church, Joyce carefully stepped over uneven ground to the roadbed shoulder where she watched the ongoing search operation. "While I was standing there, I saw another cave hole just open up in the roadbed. It was so scary to see that happen. All the kids on the Southside were really affected by what was happening," Joyce remembered. "We'd always felt so safe. It was just devastating to have three boys just disappear like that," she added.

And youthful imaginations ran wild. "Kids were always spreading rumors. There was a rumor that the boys had fallen into a cave hole that went on and on forever, just terrible stuff to hear when you're a kid," said Joyce.

Joyce walked past the roadcut site each weekday to catch the school bus, a painful reminder of Hannibal's unresolved tragedy. "Every single day I was there, I'd stop and look at what was happening. It was just surreal."

"The crying went on for days," remembers Alfred King. He and his nine siblings, children of Al and Katherine, lived on Riverside Street, which paralleled the Highway 79 roadcut. The Kings knew the three missing boys and their parents, so the grief was deep. Alfred, then eight, was a third grader at nearby Stowell School and a member of the Cub Scout pack at Southside Christian Church. "We always walked to school down the roadcut to see the construction equipment," Alfred explained, confessing that he and brothers David, Richard and Eddie also had gone into a roadbed cave a few days before Joel, Billy and Craig had vanished. "The entrance was flat to the roadbed, so we jumped in with our flashlights and candles, but it was pretty scary so we didn't go very far."

There was worry and foreboding in the air as Alfred sensed the children of Hannibal had been robbed of their innocence. "When the boys went missing, it was a big deal. The neighborhood was now scary. Our parents told us to stay away from the roadcut and the caves."

Alfred's teacher, Mrs. Drebenstedt, talked to her students about the situation and asked them to pray for the Hoag and Dowell families. "Mr. (Frederic) Kleiber, the principal, gathered students in the auditorium to talk about the unfolding situation and offer reassurance. Everyone was very upset. It was devastating for kids our age to lose friends," Alfred said.

***

Meanwhile, the 150 National Guard members activated by Governor Hearnes were on the scene as they assumed their roles in the historic drama. All weekend they'd explored a several square-mile area of the Southside, inspecting homes, garages, sheds and other outbuildings. They found many other cave openings, often in residential backyards, and these were also searched.

Another team was sent to the Continental Cement plant south of Hannibal to search the 3,500-acre plant site, including a massive limestone rock quarry and some nearby mines and caves. The quarry's limestone comprised 88 percent of the cement produced there, with other raw materials being shale, clay and iron ore.

The plant, built in the early 1900s as the Atlas Portland Cement Company, is south of Mark Twain Cave Hollow, the area where Mark Twain and friends caught gold fever, as detailed in his autobiography, from men who came through Hannibal fresh from the California gold rush in the mid-1800s.

Twain acknowledged that, aside from his fiction, there were no gold riches to be found here during his era, only dirty rocks.

But half a century later, others would discover the best limestone in the world and expand the building materials industry to Twain's hometown. The plant produced cement used to build Manhattan's Empire State Building and the Panama Canal, the historic passage connecting the Pacific Ocean with the Atlantic.

Ironically, growing regional and global competition in the cement industry in the 1960s had spurred the cement plant to join tourism promoters to advocate for a new scenic Highway 79 that went directly through Ilasco, a small company town where many cement plant workers lived.

Lieutenant Kenneth Robert Cowder was a platoon leader in the 35th MP Company when called out to report for duty. He didn't have far to travel. Cowder, twenty-nine, was a state highway department draftsman who lived on Park Avenue, less than a mile from Murphy's Cave and roadcut search locations. He'd grown up on the Southside, exploring the caves and wooded hillsides and often shooting rats with his .22 rifle at the open and smoldering city dump located at the end of Riverside Street. "Everybody in town knew these kids were missing. They didn't know exactly when or where or how, but they were just gone. So the governor felt we were the best available group for state emergency duty," Cowder explained.

The guardsmen had direct orders to coordinate with Hannibal Police and SSA President Bill Karras. "They felt that the most logical place to look and establish a search pattern was south along that range of hills along the Mississippi river. There were known caves in the area and it was pretty hilly, heavily wooded country," Cowder said.

Cowder's men organized a typical ground search, spreading out in a long line about fifteen feet apart, starting from the Murphy's Cave area near Bear Creek and heading south. They fixed their eyes to the ground as they moved slowly along looking for evidence that might provide clues to the boys' whereabouts. "We went through the hills, clear down to the cement plant area and beyond to the villages of Monkey Run and Ilasco. Then we combed the area again walking back."

One bit of evidence was discovered Saturday. A Mark Twain Emergency Squad member found a sock in the rock quarry and Craig Dowell's stepbrother, believing the sock was Craig's, ran home to find another one just like it. But the sock was a popular, widely worn brand and Karras felt there was no direct proof it was from one of the lost boys.

Cowder and his men were then dispatched to search an area north of Hannibal along River Road, a narrow ribbon of concrete that hugs the river beneath the Hannibal Lighthouse sitting high atop Cardiff Hill, the prominent high point at the north end of downtown. They searched the heavily wooded area but found nothing of significance.

National Guard Company Commander Bill Tucker, also a Hannibal native, took his team and searched Riverside Cemetery just south of the roadcut, and then spread out along Fulton Avenue west to the Mount Olivet Cemetery, less than a mile north of Mark Twain Cave. "They wanted us to do a broad sweep through this area to see if we could see any indication of the boys' whereabouts."

Tucker and his wife, Marilyn, had lived on the Southside for years, and their boys were good friends with the missing Hoag brothers. "Joey and Billy were over at our house regularly, especially Billy," Marilyn recalled. "He seemed like he needed a friend his age. Billy had called Mark, our oldest son who was the same age, several days before they disappeared and invited him to go caving. He excitedly shared that he and Joel had found a cave," Marilyn explained, "but Mark said he was grounded. Otherwise he might have gone with them."

Mystery Man

"The other aspect of this whole thing was a mystery man who was hanging out on Lover's Leap for several days before the boys were missing," Commander Tucker noted. "I know kids had been up there talking with him. He was a white guy maybe thirty or thirty-five years old, but could have been fifty, somewhere in that age range. One of the workers asked what he was doing and he said, 'I'm watching the construction activity.'"

"Back then, people did not immediately think of abduction," Tucker explained. "It was a more innocent time, and three boys would be hard to corral, especially Craig and Joel who were active and muscular, able to handle themselves."

Karras and others also had noticed this mystery man who often appeared in the early hours of the morning "standing high on a hill near the highway caves looking down on the workers. Who he was or where he came from, we never were able to discover," Karras reported, noting this individual had planted false clues (that he doesn't detail) that wasted the cavers' time.

"We don't know if this guy did anything with the boys," Tucker said, "but shortly after they disappeared workers never saw him again at the scene." Knowing this, Tucker had his men watch for any freshly dug areas where bodies could have been buried. "Especially in the cemetery near the roadcut, someone could have buried bodies in an existing grave."

"To be honest with you," Tucker added, "I thought we'd find the boys in one of the caves south of Hannibal, just over the hill that runs behind the homes along Fulton Avenue. It's not that far and they had previously explored those caves, but we didn't find a thing."

The search teams were looking hard but finding nothing days into the grueling around-the-clock search. The guardsmen conducted the foot patrols for two days, then all but twenty were released from duty.

Cowder and some of the other guardsmen were active cavers so they remained to help search Murphy's again. They donned their helmet-mounted carbide lights, and each man carried an additional flashlight as backup. Because some of the passages were so small, Cowder and the others traded baggy coveralls for snug-fitting tee shirts and blue jeans.

"We thoroughly explored and marked every passageway. Most of these passages were what we called 'finger caves,' real narrow with very little room for maneuvering. In spots, the ceiling was broken shale that had allowed moisture to seep in from the ground above, so it was muddy and wet in some areas," Cowder explained. "We dug out several more breakdown areas where the roof had caved in, but we found absolutely nothing. We couldn't find a single sign of anybody except other cavers being in that cave," Cowder explained, clearly frustrated. "There had been a tremendous number of people already through that cave by this point in the search."

At the Highway 79 roadcut site, Cowder found the geology to be a bit different from Murphy's. "You'd wiggle through an area three feet high or less and then the cave opened up with twelve, fourteen, sometimes twenty foot high ceilings, but the area you could walk through was anywhere from two feet wide to six feet wide. just narrow, narrow, narrow limestone caves."

Caver in crevice opening at the roadcut.
Photo courtesy Hannibal Courier-Post.

Cowder learned highway workers had found a makeshift ladder down in one of the roadcut openings a few days before the boys disappeared. "A few of the workers had gone down into the hole, looked left and looked right and didn't think much of it, so they discarded the ladder and filled the hole with pea gravel."

Cowder's team also searched two other caves around the hill from Murphy's that had already been searched many times. "One of them goes in about seventy-five yards, and the other goes in about twenty-five yards." Again, nothing. "We were just plowing the same ground over and over, always coming up empty."

The Mark Twain Emergency Squad extended the search to the nearby Mississippi river and several islands that dotted the muddy ribbon of water. To the north of the Memorial Bridge, McDonald, Murphy, Towhead, Turtle and Ziegler islands were carefully searched. South of the bridge, Shuck, Pearl, Tower, Fourmile and Saverton islands were explored. Nothing related to the lost boys was found, so Civil Defense Director Bill Broaddus announced dragging operations would commence. He felt the river was the only place left to search, however unlikely it was that it would provide any clues. Alas, the miles-long river search proved to be another dead end.

With a busy railroad line only a few hundred yards from the search sites, Cowder visited the Southside railroad yard near the river and secured the manifest of all the trains that had passed through Hannibal the day the boys turned up missing. "The railroad tracked down all those trains across the United States and had every one of them searched. It was a lot of work, but the railroad did that for us."

Cowder's emergency duty would last five days before he returned to his day job with the highway department, disappointed there had been no resolution to this painful mystery.

Chapter 7

Missouri - The Cave State

"There is nothing more powerful than this attraction
towards an abyss."

Jules Verne, Journey to the Center of the Earth

By the 1960s all eyes were on the heavens as the space race captured
the imagination of Americans. Space beckoned, and the moon would
be achieved before the end of the decade.

Most people likely believed that the big terrestrial discoveries
here on Earth had already been achieved. In the early twentieth
century, Robert Peary was the first to reach the North Pole in 1909,
followed by Roald Amundsen's arrival at the planet's South Pole
two years later.

Then the exploratory focus shifted from the ends of the earth
to its highest point; Mount Everest was first summited in 1953 by
Sir Edmund Hillary and Tenzing Norgay. Ocean explorers Jacques
Piccard and Don Walsh pursued the deepest ocean reaches in 1960
when they descended to the floor of the western Pacific's Mariana
Trench, a watery abyss so massive Mount Everest would fit inside.
When their submersible hit bottom in complete darkness, they were
35,800 feet below the ocean surface, lower than any man had ever
gone.

But more earthly discoveries still beckoned as cave exploration was growing as an avocation and field of scientific inquiry. Below ground, cavers enthusiastically sought completely unexplored wilderness. This subterranean world is called the *eighth continent*, an otherworldly realm that can stretch for hundreds of miles and plunge thousands of feet below the surface.

The massive and deep supercaves, of which there are only fourteen known in the world, are more rare than the highest eight thousand meter peaks of the Himalayas. Unlike mountain climbers, who can keep their summit in sight, cavers can only see the end of their path after a great investment of time and effort. These dark, wet, often tight and claustrophobic routes represent the gem of achievement, because the explorers are often going where no human has ever set foot.

The first of the discovered supercaves, Huautla, located about two hundred miles southeast of Mexico City, Mexico, initially explored in the 1960s, is the deepest cave system in the western hemisphere at 5,069 feet. Later, in 1963, Sotano de Tlamaya was discovered with a depth of 1,488 feet. Cheve Cave in Mexico is the second deepest known cave in the Americas, with a measured depth of 4,869 feet. To explore Cheve a cave team needs two kilometers of rope and the support of three underground camps.

The exciting news of exploratory achievement in Mexico helped to activate the caving gene in another generation of young men and women. As more people came into the sport during the 1960s, caving clubs, called grottos, were formed in communities across Missouri, Illinois, and other cave-rich states like Tennessee, Alabama, Georgia, called the TAG, the region with the highest concentration of caves in the world.

These cavers studied, trained, and explored, usually with the guidance of more seasoned mentors. They recognized that while caves are beautiful in their own way, heart-pounding exciting, and scientifically interesting, they remain dangerous, dark and slippery places.

Members of the St. Louis Caving Club enjoy a subterranean tour during the early 1960s when caving was growing in popularity. Author collection.

To enter a cave, they donned protective helmets with lights and entered on foot or descended with the aid of a rope. Often crawling on their knees and bellies, their lights revealing the cave's features, they moved forward into an unknown world. In some caves they discovered interesting cave formations, icicle-like stalactites hanging down from the ceiling and their stalagmite cousins growing up from the floor, receiving the eternal drips of mineralized water from above. Often the cavers emerged with muddy, wet clothing and a few abrasions.

The cavers recognized their sport required technical skills and an abundance of care and caution as they maneuvered along and over rocky, unforgiving surfaces and obstacles.

The terms *speleologist* and *spelunker* had entered the caving vocabulary nearly a century earlier. Beginning in the 1880s, caving was pioneered by Edouard-Alfred Martel who descended into and explored caves in France, England and, later, the United States. A *speleologist*, first coined in the 1890s from the French *speleologie*, defined a specialist with an interest in caves as well as study and expertise in another scientific field such as geology, hydrology or biology. The speleologist gathers data, sharing knowledge through exploration, observation and reporting.

In the 1940s, American caver Clay Perry wrote about a group of men and boys who explored caves in New England. They called themselves spelunkers and this is believed to be the first use of the term in the United States. For nearly two decades, spelunking was used to define those who embraced the avocation of cave exploration.

American spelunkers organized the National Speleological Society (NSS) in 1941 to advance the identification, exploration and conservation of US caves. Together with European cavers, these pioneers developed the techniques and tools necessary for safe cave exploration. Today the NSS has more than ten thousand registered members in an estimated 250 grottos or caving clubs around the world, promoting safety and conservation.

The *spelunker*, as described in J. Harlen Bretz's 1956 classic book *Caves of Missouri*, is primarily interested in "exploration, underground adventure and esthetic appreciation. He has no overwhelming urge to be photographed in full regalia or in difficult but readily avoidable cave situations. He has no need for newspaper or magazine publicity. Caves are fun in their own right. His greatest reward probably is in penetrating where man has never penetrated before." Bretz likely never met Bill Karras.

Many cavers now make a distinction in language, considering a *spelunker* an amateur sports caver while the term *caver* better represents those individuals with a serious, responsible approach to the sport. This contrast in definition is often captured on T-shirts and bumper stickers that read "Cavers Rescue Spelunkers."

Bretz, a University of Chicago geologist who took a special interest in Missouri caves, noted that responsible cavers are typically very concerned about cave environmentalism, the preservation of these pristine cavescapes, and their protection from the reckless intrusions of man. No longer would names be painted on cave walls or geological samples chipped off of crystallized calcite or other speleothems (formations of secondary mineral deposits) to tuck into coveralls and take home, not an uncommon behavior in past eras.

Bretz also agreed with Mark Twain who wrote, "It was an easy place to get lost in; anybody could do it." In his book *Caves of Missouri*, Bretz wrote "Getting lost in a cave is a widespread apprehension, and it certainly has some justification here, for (the cave) is a perfect labyrinth of very similar passages. Without guide, or compass, or map, or ball of string, the chance of getting lost on one's first visit would be excellent. Tom Sawyer, Becky Thatcher and especially Indian Joe could testify to this."

University of Chicago geologist J Harlen Bretz, left, is shown with with cavers Dwight Weaver (dark shirt, light pants). Tex Yokum (in cardigan), and Don Myers, right, during a 1963 tour of Mark Twain Cave. Photo courtesy Dwight Weaver.

The caves of Missouri are not supercaves. Few go below sea level, but they are still impressive karst landscapes. Explore Onondaga cave and you'll descend into a world of visual wonder. Impressive stalagmites, stalactites and active flowstones earned the cave national landmark status. These speleothems grow slowly, often taking many thousands of years to develop into what cave visitors enjoy today. These cave features are carefully protected as a single careless touch can damage or destroy them. That's why it's important to remain on established trails during cave tours to avoid any adverse impact to the cave ecosystem.

Prior to Missouri gaining statehood status in 1821, about the only attention devoted to caves was by early trappers and explorers who used them for shelter and by settlers who often utilized the cool grottos to store perishable foods during warm weather.

It was during the compilation of the state geological and natural history surveys in the 1850s that Missouri's caves entered the national spotlight. Early archaeologists found paleolithic Indian artifacts in many caves, as well as evidence of human habitation dating back ten thousand years before present.

Cave floors were found to be rich in one important resource—centuries of accumulated bat guano, which was mined for production of saltpeter, a component of gunpowder, an important necessity for hunters and pioneers forging westward across the continent.

Experts from the Smithsonian Institution and the American Museum of Natural History studied the state's flora and fauna and took special interest in cave life specimens gathered in the 1880s by Ruth Hoppin, a resident of Sarcoxie in southwestern Missouri. During this era, becoming an amateur naturalist, as Hoppin did, was a popular avocation among the upper class. She was an educator and botanist in Michigan and Massachusetts during the 1880s. After earning her Master's Degree, Hoppin served as a collector for the Harvard University Museum. She is credited with the discovery of the previously unknown Ozark cavefish (Amblyopsis rosae), the cave crayfish (Cambarus setosus Faxon), and an isopod which still bears her name (Asellus hoppinae). Most of what's known about Hoppin is found in the article *Cave Animals from Southwestern Missouri*, published in the 1889 edition of the Bulletin of Comparative Zoology.

Missourians were learning more about their natural world, and experts and novices alike were fascinated by their finds, especially the creatures that lived in the wet, pitch black cave environments. Organisms that spend their entire lives in caves are termed troglobites. These include fish, salamanders, crayfish, spiders, and insects. Specially adapted to living in complete darkness, these creatures offer great research promise for biologists. Troglobites cannot live beyond the cave, and survival may be threatened if the fragile cave environment is altered or damaged. If a damaged ecosystem is unable to regenerate, these unique creatures could face extinction.

Here's another fun term—trogloxenes. These are animals that live in caves but also return to the surface to hunt and feed. Examples of trogloxenes are bears, foxes, raccoons, packrats, swallows, and moths.

In 1852, a little girl born to pioneer parents in St. Joseph, Missouri, one of the gateways to the American West, would later make a name for herself in the state's early speleological history. Luella Agnes Owen was the first woman to explore and write about the underground world from a scholarly viewpoint. Even as a child, Luella was fascinated by her little earth treasures, the shells and fossils she found along the bluffs near her home.

Bright and naturally curious, Luella matured into a well-mannered, educated young woman thanks to the values passed along by her home-schooling mother and her father, a practicing attorney. The family maintained a large library for Luella and her two equally inquisitive sisters. Luella loved to roam the countryside and often explored caves with the help of friends. Ironically, there was not yet a single identified cave in her native Buchanan County at the time. But Luella and her two sisters shared an interest in study and travel, so she developed a broad knowledge of geology and caving, her interests fueled in part by the state geological surveys conducted earlier.

Luella would go on many cave outings wearing a long skirt and holding burning magnesium ribbons for light. She fearlessly crawled through tight passages and maneuvered past ledges and deep cracks in the cave floors. In some caves with underground streams, she would maneuver a small boat through the passages, pushing against the cave walls to propel herself forward.

Luella documented her personal cave explorations in *Cave Regions of the Ozarks and Black Hills*, published in 1898. It is a rare, difficult-to-find title, but still available today thanks to print-on-demand technology. The opening pages reflect her enthusiasm and passion for caving:

> "...the State of Missouri, and the Black Hills of South Dakota, offers exceptionally delightful regions for the study of caves or Speleology as it has been named, and the sister sciences of geology and geography at the same time... it is impossible to study either without giving attention to the other two, and therefore, instead of being separate sciences, they are the three branches of a great scientific trinity."

Owen was influenced by Dr. H. C. Hovey's 1882 book *Celebrated American Caverns,* as she quoted excerpts of his findings in her own book. She was fascinated by Hovey's description of the cave-making process:

> "Rainwater, falling amid leaves and grass, and sinking into the soil, absorbs large quantities of carbonic acid. On reaching the underlying limestone, the latter is instantly attacked by the acidulated water in which it is dissolved and carried away. It is agreed among geologists, amazing as the statement may seem, that the immense caverns of Virginia, Kentucky and Indiana, including Mammoth Cave itself... were eaten out of the solid mass of limestone by the slow, patient, but irresistible action of acidulated water."

Into the twentieth century, interest in caving continued to grow. Onondaga Cave was opened in time to be a spectacular attraction for the 1904 World's Fair in St. Louis. In 1922, archaeologist Gerard Fowke, who conducted research for several natural history organizations, published his survey of Missouri caves in *Bulletin 76 of the Smithsonian Institute, Bureau of American Ethnology.*

The number of Missouri caves continued to increase annually as new discoveries were made by landowners developing their properties. By 1940, the Missouri Geological Survey, under the leadership of staff cave enthusiast Willard Farrar, had identified 210 caves in forty counties. Farrar's excellent field work would inform Bretz's later explorations and study. Farrar's dedication ended too soon; he was killed in New Guinea during World War II.

By the time Bretz, the geologist and pipe-smoking academic at the University of Chicago, published his classic book in 1956, 437 caves had been identified in fifty-five Missouri counties.

As of 2017, Missouri has more than 7,300 identified caves in eighty-three counties, second only to Tennessee. Much progress has been made in the past six decades to identify and map these wild karst landscapes, thanks to the efforts of a generation of cave and conservation professionals, including: Frank Dahlgren, a St. Louis caver and machinist; Dr. Oscar "Oz" Hawksley, Central Missouri State University conservationist; and geologist Jerry Vineyard who would later become the contemporary "Father of Missouri Caving" and serve for many years as deputy state geologist with the Missouri Department of Natural Resources. These men, looking to build upon Bretz's work, established the Missouri Speleological Survey in 1956 to locate, explore, study and conserve Missouri's caves.

In an article about Bretz's Missouri research and explorations, published in *Missouri Speleology Volume 19 3-4 1979*, Jerry Vineyard wrote: "It is appropriate to refer to Bretz as the 'father' of speleology in Missouri because he approached the subject not as a young man, but at a time when most men would have been considering retirement." While his age tempered his cave exploration, Bretz's passion and findings inspired a generation of young cavers who continued his work. The Missouri Speleological Survey's cave files represent one of the nation's most comprehensive collections of cave data in the United States.

These modern cave experts agreed with their predecessors that long before Missouri was a state, the region was an ideal "cave factory," as Vineyard described, with layers of carbonate rock and plentiful rainfall and lush vegetation to create the acidic chemical soup that percolates through the soil, dissolving rock and creating cavities and tunnels as it moves between geologic layers. The caves formed in Missouri's limestone and dolomite geological strata may stretch for miles, but seldom go very deep into the earth; most remain at or above sea level. Marvel Cave in Stone County is the deepest, with a depth of 383 feet. The vast majority of Missouri caves are in the southern half of the state where the geology especially favors cave formation.

Perry County, located in Southeast Missouri, is the hollowest, most cave-rich area in the state. Half a century ago, this county had only forty-four recorded caves. Since then, nearly seven hundred caves have been identified, more than any other Missouri county. Here you'll find the state's longest cave, Crevice Cave, which has been surveyed for nearly thirty-one miles. Neighboring Berome Moore Cave has more than eighteen miles of mapped passages.

***

On a late summer day in 1963, six boys found an uncharted Perry County Cave and launched an adventure they would never forget. The six—Wallie Brieg, Lee Lottes, Mick Paulus, Gary Schnurbusch, Mike Vogel, and Ronnie Zahner—explored a cave entrance that had recently been exposed by heavy rains on the Prevallet farm near Perryville.

Equipped with flashlights, fishing line, candles and candy bars, the boys, who were no strangers to cave exploration, wriggled through the narrow opening. They had tied the fishing line to a nearby gate and let it out behind them as they moved through the cave.

The boys soon found themselves in a large room where Lee placed one of their candles to help illuminate the way. Minutes later they encountered a three-foot gap in the muddy cave floor. The boys carefully took turns jumping over the breach. When Wallie was about to jump, another boy knocked a rock into the dark maw. "It took a five-count to hit the bottom," Wallie told a reporter, figuring it was a good fifty or sixty feet deep.

The boys journeyed onward, moving horizontally and downward until they reached a flat area with walls more than one hundred feet high. "You could drive a trailer-truck through it," Wallie explained.

Soon, the six boys had exhausted their supply of candles and fishing line, but they continued forward, nimbly stepping on jagged stepping stones to traverse a waterway. By now, the boys were starting to get worried. Mick Paulus assessed their situation; things were not looking good—their candles had burned out, and the flashlights were growing dim. If they continued to descend, he thought, it meant they were less likely to be able to find their way out.

Nervously traversing a ledge above the water, Lee slipped and fell into the cold water, chest high. The mishap seriously spooked the boys who were already cold, exhausted and feeling lost. They realized time was ebbing away. After three hours of travel, a sobering thought settled upon the boys—*we may not make it out.*

Taking a break to rest, they turned their lights off to conserve battery power while they refueled their stomachs with candy bars. After a long ten minutes in the pitch-black cave, the lights were switched on and the boys felt a renewed determination to escape the cave's chilling grip.

The boys entered another large room where Wallie noticed an opening high on the wall. "I decided to climb up there and found it was like a flat area with another ceiling." Wallie explored farther but retreated when he saw a long shadow cast across the wall. "It reminded me of a giant spider web." Wallie ignored his fears and returned to the ledge. With gloved hands he grabbed the spider web only to discover it was the fishing line they had unspooled earlier in the day. The boys were jubilant and quickly followed the line back to the surface where their odyssey had started hours earlier.

"That was our last cave," Wallie said. Micky nodded agreement, saying he never went into another cave after the scary experience. The six 1960s cavers had stumbled upon what would later be named Moore Cave, extending nearly seventeen miles beneath Perry County, another unique and beautiful subterranean world.

One of the six cavers has since died, but most of the others still live in Perry County or nearby. None of the explorers ever set foot in another cave. "Oh Lord, it was one hell of a day," Lee exclaimed. (Based on a story by reporter Amanda Keefe and published in the Perryville Republic-Monitor, December 12, 2013)

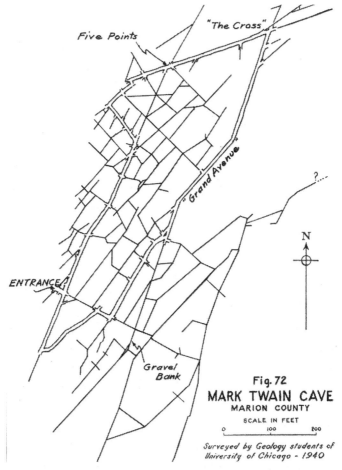

Map of Mark Twain Cave, courtesy Linda Coleberd.

The Hannibal area offers a real caving distinction; four of the state's relatively few maze caves are located here: Mark Twain Cave, Cameron Cave, LaBaume Cave, and Murphy's Cave. A maze cave poses special challenges because of its extraordinarily complex and confusing criss-cross layout. This complexity makes it very dangerous. Imagine for a moment you are exploring a city with a grid of hundreds of intersecting streets, each with largely identical scenery every step of the way. Walk around for a while and you'll quickly lose orientation and become hopelessly lost. Or, walk far into a cornfield on a cloudy night, close your eyes and spin around several times. Now, which way do you walk to return to your car?

Mark Twain Cave is the best-known cave in northeast Missouri and the state's first commercial show cave, visited annually by thousands of tourists drawn here by history and Mark Twain's memorable stories about the adventures of Tom Sawyer, Huckleberry Finn and Becky Thatcher. The cave covers twelve acres with 2.82 miles of passages.

The cave was first discovered during the snowy winter of 1819-20 by settler Jack Simms while pursuing a panther. Since it was late in the day, Simms returned the next day with his brothers, Roderick and William, and a friend J. H. Buchanan. The foursome brought their dogs and guns and followed the panther's tracks to an opening in the hillside. The dogs led the way, and their barks grew fainter as the men hurriedly squeezed into the cave and took in the wonder before them—branching passageways with high ceilings, and a relatively balmy fifty-two-degree environment compared to the cold outside. Over the years, the cave had various names, such as Panther Cave and Saltpeter Cave, due to the presence of bat guano rich in saltpeter, a main component of gunpowder.

The cave developed a dark reputation in the 1840s when it was purchased by St. Louis surgeon Dr. Joseph Nash McDowell. In medical school back in Kentucky years earlier, McDowell had grown interested in research about the preservation qualities of bat guano, a raw material found in abundance in many caves. He visited what was then called Saltpeter Cave and found it to be a perfect underground laboratory for his curious research. During this time,

McDowell struggled to obtain a cadaver for his research, but he soon had bittersweet success after one of his ten children, a fourteen-year-old daughter, died after a terrible illness. Her poor body was enclosed in a copper cylinder, filled with alcohol and suspended in one of the dismal cave passages.

It was during this era when McDowell Cave attracted the interest of Samuel Clemens and his buddies who spent much of their free time playing in the cave. Although McDowell had placed a sturdy gate across the entrance, the curious boys found another way in and would fearlessly lift the girl's body up by the hair to have a closer look at the preserved corpse. This macabre adventure thankfully ended after alarmed residents learned of the bizarre experiment underway and demanded McDowell stop the research and remove the girl's body from the cave.

When McDowell died in 1868, Zachariah Fielder and R. H. Stilwell, who owned the nearby Hannibal Brick Plant, purchased the Hannibal cave with big plans for the property. The park soon offered the conveniences of a resort: a dance hall, baseball park, swings and hammocks, pure mineral-rich water promoted as a healthful tonic, and a horse-racing track.

After Mark Twain published The Adventures of Tom Sawyer in 1876, the cave became a popular tourist attraction. John East, a Cave Hollow resident, started a guide service making Mark Twain Cave Missouri's first commercial show cave, in continuous service ever since.

In 1890, East dynamited out the entrance still used today. In 1900, the cave property was bought by John S. Mainland who enjoyed a robust tourist trade thanks to development of good roads from town.

Judge Evan T. Cameron, who had worked as a cave guide in his youth, purchased the 265-acre Mark Twain Cave property in 1923 and electrified the cave's public passages in 1939. Today, the limestone walls and ceilings that tourists see during cave tours still exhibit the dark smudges made by the smoke from torches used by Jack Simms and many others during earlier explorations. The cave ownership and management remains in the family.

Across Cave Hollow was another speleological gem that had never been seen by human eyes until discovered by Cameron's son,

Archie, in 1935. On a cold February morning, he was checking the lifestock when he noticed steam from moist, warmer air coming from a sinkhole. A few days later Cameron and his helpers enlarged the sink and entered, becoming the first humans to see this remarkable virgin cave. They named it Cameron Cave, a spectacular eighteen-acre maze network with 4.62 miles of passages. Cameron offers a more complex adventure, with its miles of winding passages that serve as a warning for the uninitiated caver. The cave is not electrified so any explorers must have adequate lighting and spare batteries during guided tours.

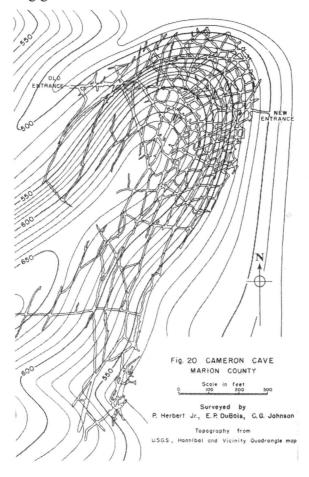

Map of Cameron Cave, courtesy Linda Coleberd.

161

Less than a mile from Mark Twain Cave, between Cave Hollow and Saverton, is LaBaume Cave discovered by Captain Alfred Bulkey in 1830. Due to a geological uplift, the entrance to the cave is high up a hillside facing the Mississippi River. When first discovered, the entrance was very narrow so Bulkey dynamited the opening to enlarge it.

In the early twentieth century, LaBaume was quarried from above for Burlington Limestone for Atlas Portland cement production and mined below for shale, making exploration very dangerous. Blasting and ongoing operations took a toll, resulting in breakdowns in several cave passages. A 1965 report concluded, "This cave is not open to exploration due to its unstable condition."

A long-time controversy centers on whether LaBaume and Mark Twain Caves were once connected. A 1912 *Hannibal Courier-Post* newspaper article reported that landowner Peter A. LaBaume "made the interesting discovery that the two caves are connected and although their openings are less than two miles distant, the passage from entrance to entrance winds about for more than four miles." Most cavers now believe that while the two caves were possibly connected long ago, passageways have since filled with silt, and changes to the topography have likely severed any direct connections between the caves.

***

Clearly, caving is not for the armchair enthusiast. It's a hands-on avocation; you need to be highly focused, well trained, and embrace a stewardship ethic. You might be the first human to ever set foot in a particular cave, as Archie Cameron did, and witness its unique environment. Cavers are quick to tell you that caves are delicate ecosystems that are always full of air, water, or a mixture of both. And the balance of nature's elements determines the health of the cave and the robustness of its ecosystem. Caves created eons ago remain fragile, always changing environments that can face substantial degradation due to reckless human exploration. So cavers wear another hat, that of environmental advocate.

With this rich underground classroom below their neighborhood, it was only natural for three inquisitive boys to be attracted to the mysterious underground. It was a veritable laboratory for adventure and learning. But curiosity led to a darker fate as the three boys, who shared a dangerous mix of characteristics, remained lost. With the fearlessness of teenage boys, and lacking any technical caving skills, they had dismissed the serious risk as their grand adventure had beckoned them onward—Hannibal's own version of the abyss.

Chapter 8

Growing Despair, A Mother's Plea

"We Love You, Please Come Home."

On Sunday evening, May 14, Karras tried a new strategy as he sought more clues to the boys' whereabouts. In an effort to find the lost boys, Mr. and Mrs. Hoag spoke via a nationwide television appeal coordinated by a Quincy television station.

"Joey... Joey, Billy, this is Mother's Day. Please come home and make it a good Mother's Day," Helen pleaded into the television camera. "I had a good supper for you tonight. Your brothers and sisters all love you and have been looking so hard for you. Please come home before I have a heart attack," Mrs. Hoag begged, her face streaked with tears and deeply lined with fatigue.

Mr. Mike Hoag offered a father's desperate appeal to the boys: "If you hear, will you please come home or call, and we'll come and get you. We love you, but we have to get to you real quick and get you home."

Just before noon the next morning, a solid clue found its way to Hannibal thanks to the television broadcast. An Overland, Missouri construction worker on the Interstate 55 project east of the St. Louis area called the Rescue Control headquarters number he'd seen on television the night before. Louis Guerra reported seeing two boys fitting the descriptions of Joel Hoag and Craig Dowell at a workhouse in the South Broadway area of St. Louis Monday morning. He told authorities the boys had asked him for directions to suburban Ferguson, Missouri. Guerra reportedly said he was confident the two boys were Joel and Craig because he remembered their photos in the newspaper, adding that both boys appeared "very, very dirty." But Guerra told police he'd seen no signs of a third boy. According to newspaper reports, the Missouri State Highway Patrol dispatched crews who later found two boys, but they were the wrong boys—two nineteen-year-olds from Cape Girardeau, Missouri.

Cavers gather outside Rescue Control for a search update. Photo courtesy Hannibal Courier-Post.

Hannibal Mayor Harry Musgrove, nervous about the national attention for his community, continued to believe the boys were not lost underground. "I don't feel the boys are in the caves. I think they are in some other place," Musgrove told reporters. "They could be out having some fun. That's our only hope now. I'm more inclined to believe they ran away." He added, "If we keep this vigil up, the kids might never come back. You can't come back when you have two hundred or three hundred people looking for you."

But others were skeptical of Musgrove's view. Craig Dowell's aunt, Betty LeFever, told the authorities Craig had not run away because he'd changed trousers after school, and his money was still in the pants pocket.

Bill Tucker, commander of the 2175th MP Company, who led the ground search in Hannibal, was a career military man with good instincts. He doubted the boys left the Hannibal area on their own. "We knew those boys. They just ran the hills near their house. They were Tom Sawyers and liked to do adventurous things. They didn't have a lot of parental supervision because the parents were working at the tavern, so they were on their own a lot. But they were good kids not likely to run off. They always came home for supper."

***

Tensions were running high during the second week of the search. The frantic, non-stop efforts fueled by exhaustion created some short fuses among search team members. Mayor Musgrove met with Karras and his team to resolve the growing schism between out-of-town cavers and local searchers. Musgrove announced that Karras' team would handle all below-ground search activities, and the Mark Twain Rescue Squad would manage all surface search operations, with Musgrove and Civil Defense Director Bill Broaddus coordinating the efforts.

Suddenly, the flame of hope flickered Monday when a fresh lead emerged in the search. Two neighborhood playmates of the boys came forward to confirm how Joel, Billy and Craig had been playing a dangerous game in the Lover's Leap area, eluding construction workers and climbing into the cave openings exposed by road crews. The boys identified the general area where the lost boys had entered, and cavers found a section of a cave passage filled with shale that appeared to have been from a recent ceiling collapse. If the boys were trapped, cavers hoped they might still have enough air and still be alive. Cavers began digging operations to remove the ceiling breakdown and reopen the passage. It was tedious work as the weary cave crew labored through the night.

In the early morning hours, they finally emerged from below the roadcut to report to the town that they had found no sign of the lost boys.

When eighth grader Gary Rush exited the school bus on Monday afternoon, May 15, he found search leader Bill Karras waiting nearby in an idling jeep. Karras wanted to know more about other areas where the Southside boys liked to explore. Rush jumped into Karras' jeep and the duo roared off down the roadcut, turning left onto the steep route up to Lover's Leap. Named for an incident when an Indian maiden supposedly leaped to her death for her love, Lover's Leap stands three hundred feet above the river. The jutting rocky point, its distinguishing feature, is all that remains from an 1858 slide when a large limestone mass calved off and slid down the steep slope.

"I showed Karras the concave lair beneath and just to the north of the rocky point where we'd gathered from time to time growing up, but it wasn't very deep into the cliff and nothing was found," Rush said. Rush also showed Karras some cave openings farther south that were added to the list of areas to search.

Members of the Hoag family and their neighbors maintained a steady vigil at the scene. SSA President Bill Karras and Conway Christensen, his vice president, would walk to the Hoag's nearby home each evening to brief them on the day's activities. The families and the rest of Hannibalians held tightly to hope, but there was never any good news from the caver leaders.

Still, the families maintained great trust in the seasoned cavers who were leading the search to find their sons. "Karras was right for the job," said Fred Hoag. "You needed someone who was articulate and comfortable with the media to be a spokesman, and that was him. Karras handled every aspect well. I had no hard feelings toward Bill Karras in any way." Hoag pointed out that the St. Louis Hondo Grotto group led by Conway Christenson was equally qualified, and highly respected, often being tapped to work in huge show caves, doing mapping work and laying electrical lines in a way that maintained the integrity of the fragile karst

168

environments. "These guys were good. They were knowledgeable and experienced and helped write the book on a lot of this stuff," Hoag added.

As in more normal times, the Hoag household with its eleven children was a natural gathering place. Lynnie had quit her job to devote full attention to the cave search. The family members would slump home after a long day at the cave sites, emotionally exhausted. "You had to hold onto hope," said a Hoag daughter, "but our emotions would just go up and down like a rollercoaster. Four or five of us would just collapse on a double bed with our clothes on and fall right to sleep. It all seemed so surreal."

As Lynnie lay on the bed one evening, she reflected darkly. This once idyllic neighborhood, brimming with children, was suddenly cast into the shadows of despair and worry. Lynnie's mind wandered as she recalled a childhood memory involving a spooky elderly neighbor who lived on nearby Union Street. "My girlfriends would tell me about all of the interesting pictures he had on a wall in his living room. I was curious, so I went to his house to see, expecting to find photos of horses or bunnies, dogs and cats, but it was child porn," she exclaimed. "He was a pedophile, with tons of pictures of boys and girls and adults. He came up behind me and put his hand on my shoulder, but I wiggled free and ran out of the house. Dirty old man, and he had a wife, too!"

It's unclear if the man was ever reported to the police, but he took his darkness and moved from the neighborhood years before the boys went missing.

Karen Townes, a student at Hannibal High School in 1967, spent a lot of time at the Hoag house during the search. Karen was going steady with Tim Hoag, and his sister, Debbie, was Karen's best friend. "Debbie and I would climb out her bedroom window onto the roof and sunbathe. It was so much fun. I was over there all the time and knew the whole family very well."

Townes was swept up in the family's grief and had her own way of coping and helping the family. She went home, gathered up her childhood collection of dolls, and brought them back for little Denise Hoag, the youngest child. "I just wanted to give, to do something for the family to put a smile on their faces."

Friends were constantly coming to the Hoag house to offer support or to bring a meal for the beleaguered family. "When anyone came to the door, there would be tears and hugs and wailing by Mrs. Hoag. Mr. Hoag didn't express his emotion so openly. He was more supportive of the others. It was very stressful for someone my age. I was fifteen at the time," Townes explained.

Townes described a household awash with grief and desperation during long evenings spent with the family. "They were getting phone calls all night long. I remember Mrs. Hoag being so exhausted she'd go lie down in the bedroom across from the living room. She'd wake up crying and screaming, and Mr. Hoag would go in and comfort her. Everyone was exhausted, it was chaotic, just very painful. Yet, we were always hoping for some answers or that the boys would come back."

Desperate for answers, the family saw promise in every lead, no matter how unusual. "It was devastating during the search," Townes recalled. "Mrs. Hoag was putting her hope in anything that came along. A woman psychic from overseas called one night and told Mrs. Hoag to go up to the top of Lover's Leap, open up the Bible to a certain scripture, and the boys would come down out of the sky. And I said, 'Mrs. Hoag you don't believe that do you?' But she did it. She was willing to do anything to get those boys back."

News of the Hannibal crisis had made its way around the world. And several other psychics added their prognostications. A clairvoyant and bespeckled parapsychologist in Utrecht, Holland, Gerard Croiset, said he'd studied maps and newspaper clippings and had a vision of the Murphy's Cave entrance. He claimed the boys would be located at a "sharp dropoff in one of three passages leading from the entrance," reported the Associated Press. The Mark Twain Rescue Squad was again dispatched to make yet another check of the cave but found no sharp drop-offs nor any new evidence. Croiset had often been tapped by police in missing person cases overseas, but authenticated successes were few and judged no better than chance.

Another psychic felt the boys would be found about twenty-six feet from a piece of heavy equipment, but this zone fell within the roadcut area covered over and over again by cavers in recent days.

One of America's best-known psychics, Jeane Dixon, reviewed news clippings about the lost youngsters and visited Hannibal. Dixon, widely known for her syndicated newspaper column, had been born Lydia Emma Pinckert in Medford, Wisconsin sixty-three years earlier. While growing up in southern California, Dixon claimed a gypsy seer had read her palm and predicted she would herself become a famous seer.

The lost boys' families hoped she could tell them if their sons had been abducted. When Dixon arrived at the roadcut, she was drawn to the Lover's Leap hill towering overhead but couldn't offer anything more detailed. "The psychics seemed to feel uneasy about Hannibal with all its caves. They felt it was unstable, sitting on this massive cave system," said Lynnie Hoag.

Still another psychic had a vision of the boys in a railroad car loaded with oranges. Yet another seer sensed the boys were in a railcar with the word Louisiana prominent in her mind's eye, unclear whether that represented the state or the community near Hannibal.

The SSA's Karras reported the Rescue Control operations center had heard from seven clairvoyants. He said some of them sensed the boys might be in the general area of Riverside Cemetery just south of the roadcut site. But none could offer any more specific information. The cemetery and the nearby city dump, located at the end of Riverside Street, were carefully searched many times during the search operation, both by local volunteers and National Guardsmen.

The carnival-like atmosphere continued when a diviner arrived to locate the boys. He told Karras he would demonstrate his divining technique using a coat hanger with a piece of meat attached to one end. The man was politely asked to go home.

***

Late one evening, one of the Hoag girls went into Joel's room and sat on his bed. They all missed the boys terribly, and the pain was almost too much to bear. Sitting on a side table was a drawing Joel had made of a UFO he claimed to have seen over Lover's Leap the previous August. She picked up the sheet of paper, held it close and smiled.

Joel loved astronomy and had received a telescope for Christmas. Always looking toward the heavens, Joel Hoag had raced home one evening the previous summer and excitedly told his family about seeing the UFO. His drawing shows a cylindrical object with legs at each end. The Hoag's neighbor lady revealed she too had seen a similar UFO hovering over Lover's Leap and told the Hoags it "scared her."

Here is the description Joel dictated to a sister who wrote it down in his school notebook:

> On the early morning hours of August 2, 1966 I spotted some (sic) Extraterrestrial object. I have never seen anything like it before. It seemed to be transparent with... lights within. It was going about 20 to 30 miles per hour. It didn't make a sound so it couldn't have been a plane of any sort. And there wasn't but the slightest puff of wind to hold up a glider and it wouldn't be very smart to fly a glider in the dark anyway. It could have been a balloon but I doubt it. It had a polished surface. How do I know this. I will tell you. It was a perfect sphere and it looked like the hard plastic you get in a model car [kit]... I determined it to be an inch thick or more. If it had been a balloon it would toss around a lot. This thing moves in a dead center direction. I believe it to be southeast. And the big mystery is that there was Gibbous Moon (less than full). At first I saw the glare of the moon on it then all of a sudden the light went out within and the glare stopped. I believe that whatever source this thing came from had a way

of stopping reflection and adding transparency
[so] you could not see it in the sky. That is my
story.   Joel Hoag

The Hannibal cave search was unfolding during an unusual time. During the period 1966-1967, there was a major UFO flap in America. Many thousands of sightings of unidentified flying objects were reported coast to coast to local police departments, media organizations, military bases and aviation authorities. People were looking skyward and observing strange things and unusual movements that seemed to defy conventional explanations.

Thousands of startling incidents were reported. Illuminated flying objects that neither looked nor acted like conventional aircraft were seen. Cars or trucks would reportedly stall during these incidents as if the electrical systems had been temporarily disabled. Some witnesses claimed they saw UFOs landing or hovering near the ground. They heard strange noises and saw powerful beams of light from overhead. Some experiencers claimed they saw unearthly beings, while others reported physiological effects such as odd sunburns, disorientation and lost time after their sightings.

In Michigan, there was a rash of sightings of hovering balls of light being reported night after night. In the end, these Michigan UFO sightings were explained away as swamp gas, a theory soundly rejected by most of the eyewitnesses. Newspapers around the country carried these sensational stories on the front pages.

The flurry of public fear and escalating concern prompted calls for congressional hearings into this disturbing phenomenon. The significance of this rash of sightings is that it occurred while an investigation of the UFO phenomenon was underway by the University of Colorado UFO Project. This probe, which studied only a fraction of the total number of cases reported, fell short of shedding any real understanding on the causes and sources of these sightings.

What was happening? Were these objects weather balloons, solid, physical flying crafts, or some interdimensional phenomenon?

Russian weapons? Or were they products of overactive imaginations feeding a developing mass hysteria? There were many questions, but few answers.

There were numerous UFO sightings during this period in the Hannibal-Quincy area. A Quincy couple was driving home from Hannibal on a spring afternoon when the driver looked off to the left along the forested border of the fertile bottomland east of the Mississippi River. Over the trees, he noticed a large cigar-shaped object hovering motionless perhaps 200-300 yards away. He quickly commented to his wife, and she clearly saw the object, too. The driver pulled the car onto the shoulder of Highway 57, and the couple got out so they could safely keep their eyes fixed on the object.

By now, several other cars had pulled over and the drivers and passengers also were watching the UFO with a mixture of fear and wonder. The group of eyewitnesses along rural Highway 57 agreed the mysterious object looked like a giant cigar. One man suggested the object had the appearance of two dinner plates or saucers placed together and then viewed from the side in profile. "We all watched the object for fifteen minutes or so," explained one eyewitness, "when suddenly it just vanished, as if you'd hit a light switch. There was no sensation of movement. It didn't take off, it was just here one second and gone the next."

A short time later, a teenage Hannibal girl was waiting with her brother for the school bus one spring morning. She suddenly noticed something in her peripheral vision, and when she glanced back at their house a shiny, silvery disk was seen hovering about twenty feet above the rooftop. She gasped in surprise and grabbed her brother's jacket sleeve to get his attention.

"Look!" The siblings stood in silence, frozen in fear, taking in the scene. "It looked solid and just hung there in the air. We watched it for a few minutes and then, just as the school bus rounded the corner down the street, it vanished all of a sudden. There was no zipping off or flying away. It was just instantly gone." The sober, Christian woman, now in her sixties, says she remembers the incident clearly and still maintains it happened just as she described. She remains mystified by the strange encounter.

These unusual sightings and the larger national phenomenon left citizens, law enforcement, and military authorities scratching their heads. While there was never any effort to connect the missing boys with this strange flurry of UFO sightings across Missouri and the nation, it did add another chilling and mysterious dimension to the Hannibal search.

***

Late the second week of the search, Dad and I were back at the scene. We joined the growing crowd of onlookers lining Birch Street and caught the pronounced stench of decomposition that hung thick in the humid evening air. We knew the dozens of other curiosity-seekers were thinking the worst, too. *Is that the smell of death?*

A cave searcher stopped briefly to take a drink from his canteen, then told us the odor was likely from a sewer line damaged by the road construction or a dead animal in the surrounding woods.

Woody St. Clair, a member of the Mark Twain Emergency Squad, said a local funeral director and the Marion County Coroner were called to the scene and both men believed the odor was not from human decomposition, most likely a dog or raccoon dead in the woods. But St. Clair wasn't so confident. "Over the years, we recovered a lot of dead bodies and the smell of human decomposition is a sickening 'sweet' odor. That's what I smelled that day at Murphy's Cave. And keep in mind, that odor can make its way through soil."

The odor fed everyone's worst fears and seemed to further strengthen the resolve of the heroic searchers. The cavers were still searching as fatigue and frustration took a terrible toll, but one could tell the operation was winding down, a victim of its own lack of momentum. "We'd looked everywhere. We still had volunteers, but had no place to send them. We'd exhausted every lead," said Joe Tripodi who helped coordinate Rescue Control.

Tripodi said even the very smallest of avenues in the caves were tackled by a caver very slight of build. "This one guy was pushing these caves to the point where he couldn't wear his helmet. He was squeezing into the smallest, tight passageways, so we truly exhausted every possible lead."

The national media outlets were constantly asking Tripodi in Rescue Control for any new information.

"Do you think you're going to find anything?"

"Do you have any fresh leads?"

"They were frustrated because they'd photographed and filmed the same scenes many times. I told them we'd exhausted all leads and ran out of places to look. So they packed up and left," Tripodi said.

Gone were the Associated Press and United Press International wire service reporters and photographers who had fed stories and images to thousands of newspapers coast to coast for two weeks. The LIFE magazine photographer, who had documented the search for the leading national newsweekly of the era, packed up his gear and left too.

Volunteer search personnel reluctantly began to give notice so they could return to their jobs. And Tobin Construction's crews were more than ready to resume the highway construction, now well behind schedule.

The search had already cost nearly one million dollars in equipment, supplies and man-hours. Now, only a dozen or so dog-tired cavers were still on the job, and they operated with a greatly reduced sense of urgency. "There's no reason to hurry now," said Tex Yokum, acknowledging the worst fears. If the boys were underground, they were deceased after more than a week.

Yokum and the others were still searching for an elusive cave passage, so he ordered the two hundred-foot-long roadbed trench, fifty feet wide and eight feet deep, extended another fifty feet in a final effort to identify the location of any more passages. "And if we don't find them there, I'm going home," Yokum told a reporter. Karras agreed. "If the kids aren't in it, that will just about be it."

Bill Karras, right, during the Hannibal search. Photo courtesy Quincy Herald-Whig.

On Thursday, May 18, after this final search failed to turn up any clues, Karras released a statement to city leaders announcing that search operations would end at five p.m. By then, Karras said, all leads, caves, tunnels and passages had been checked. "There will be no other place to go," he told officials. Mayor Harry Musgrove and Bill Bridges, vice-commander of the Mark Twain Emergency Squad, said they would keep the squad, civil defense, auxiliary police and the Red Cross and Salvation Army on standby should resources be needed.

Mayor Musgrove expressed gratitude for the outpouring of support and help during Hannibal's darkest time. "Words are inadequate to thank the many units and volunteers that have aided in the search." Bridges echoed the sentiment, adding a reference to the Vietnam War underway. "Every day, mothers receive word that their sons are missing in action. Those three were active boys, and we deeply regret that they, also, are missing in action. They are missing

177

in action, but not lost."

Karras informed the community he'd found a homemade ladder in the Hoag's basement, the one believed to have been used by the boys to gain entry to the roadbed cave before they disappeared. Red clay mud samples from the ladder proved the boys had used it in the caves in the Lover's Leap road cut during previous explorations but not on the day they vanished.

Karras arranged for several cavers from the Hondo rescue team to remain in Hannibal to pursue any new leads, despite the fact all efforts to date had found no evidence of the boys' whereabouts. Karras continued to suspect the boys had been trapped in a sealed off tunnel or buried in a collapse not evident to cavers who had searched the narrow caves below the roadbed and the Lover's Leap roadcut.

The other reason for scaling back the search was the condition of the caves, now considered very dangerous. Tex Yokum and three other cavers narrowly escaped a collapse as they had exited Murphy's Cave. Just seconds after they passed, several tons of rock and shale came down, blocking the passage and entrance. Murphy's Cave, which had been open for more than three weeks, was drying out and cavers considered it increasingly dangerous with a growing risk of additional ceiling collapses. "By then, the cave was *very* unstable," Tripodi said. "Our people had pushed it as far as they felt comfortable. We didn't want to lose any more lives trying to find what at that point would have been remains. That's when we decided to pull out of Murphy's Cave. It was beyond reasonable to send people in there."

There was no more digging to be done at the roadcut. Any digging beyond the state right-of-way would quickly become problematic. "We couldn't dig everywhere," Tripodi said, "because you would need permissions for private property, and you'd have to drill and blast through rock. Then you'd start breaking windows and foundations, so it really became almost impossible to consider the option."

Milton Martin, one of the local searchers who had helped search Murphy's Cave the evening of May 10, spoke for all Hannibal residents when he expressed the frustration and disappointment of a community. "It's just a damn tragedy. I think they were under the roadbed, and there was a cave-in and they couldn't get out. If they lost their flashlight, they would be in total darkness, complete blackness. There's no way they could find their way out."

John Janes, one of the last people to see the lost boys going into Murphy's Cave the afternoon of May 10, couldn't believe the search was winding down. "It's just amazing they weren't found." Janes believes the boys are entombed in Murphy's. "We'll never know, but I think they're still there. I saw 'em go in and that's it."

Howard Hoffmaster, editor of the *Hannibal Courier-Post*, and his seven-person staff had worked long hours during the search. "Never had a story quite like this," Hoffmaster said years later, adding that the story haunted him for a decade. "It was a complete mystery." He initially believed the boys had run off or were just running late. Later in the search, Hoffmaster became convinced the missing trio was likely trapped underground, somewhere.

Bill Owen, whose two brothers, Ed and Ron, had been lost for much of a day in Murphy's Cave in June 1961, found the search bringing back memories about his good friend Joel Hoag. "He liked doing a lot of different things. Joel daydreamed a lot in school, always looking out the window on nice days. The teacher would come up and tap him on the shoulder to get his attention. He just loved the outdoors. He was a good kid. He gave me half of his allowance for a while because I didn't get one. That's a pretty good kid who does that."

The grieving process continued as people remembered, reflected, and found comfort in the memories.

On Friday, May 19, Bill Karras boarded a government C-9A aircraft in St. Louis and departed for his Virginia farm where he lived with his wife, Janelle. Karras reported 150 cavers had searched 247 caves, fissures and other features. While local townspeople were grateful for the effort by the cavers and scores of other volunteers, there was still no resolution for the fright and grief that continued to grip them. "If I could just find out one way or the other," said Helen Dowell. "It's a terrible thing not to know if your son is alive or dead."

The next day, a technician from a Palo Alto, California firm arrived with a Magnachrometer, a device used to locate metal buried underground. It had been used successfully to find skiers after an avalanche. Search personnel used the device inside the caves to try and find the small shovel the boys reportedly had with them, but the effort was unsuccessful.

Mayor Musgrove, who was as concerned about the lost boys as he was the growing and unwelcome national attention, announced that after the search was completed all wild cave openings within the city limits would be closed. Thousands of tourists visited Hannibal, and he wanted to assure them the community was safe to visit. He lamented all the kids who had been lost in the caves across the decades. The fearful trail led back to the previous century when Twain's Tom Sawyer and Becky Thatcher emerged from a cave as they escaped from Injun Joe. American literature had fed the imaginations of generations of children, many of whom had acted boldly at great risk in a way Twain could never have anticipated. Musgrove was committed to ensuring no more kids would be lost in the caves.

Musgrove had only to look to the national media to see the picture being painted of Hannibal. LIFE magazine, in the May 26, 1967 issue, ran a short story with a photo of a caver in a maze cave passage. The story angle was fully focused on the Mark Twain literary angle and failed to convey the seriousness and scope of the search.

Searching a Cave for Three Tom Sawyers

In one of the caves that honeycomb the hills near the Mississippi River in Mark Twain's hometown of Hannibal, MO—like the one in which Tom Sawyer and his girlfriend Becky Thatcher got lost—a rescue worker searched through a dark grotto. Some 150 volunteers joined the hunt.

In a Tom Sawyer adventure of their own, three Hannibal boys–Billy Hoag, eleven, his brother Joey, thirteen, and Craig Dowell, fourteen—had gone into the cave to explore and had vanished. It recalled Becky's words: "Tom, Tom, we're lost! We're lost! We never can get out of this awful place."

Where could these three modern day Tom Sawyers be? Most of the experienced cavers believed the boys were beneath the Highway 79 roadbed, somehow missed—incredibly—by scores of cavers who crawled through the subterranean cave system for many days. How could this happen?

Here's one theory supported by seasoned cavers Jerry Vineyard, Joe Tripodi and Tex Yokum, as related by Tripodi. "After talking with Jerry and Tex later, we remembered finding red clay instead of shale on the ceiling in spots, as well as the floor, and we think what might have happened is the boys went down into the cave, and everything was kind of unstable from the blasting and they got into one of these weakened areas with clay for the ceiling. Maybe they disturbed the ceiling, perhaps with the shovel, and it came down and crushed them. During the search, we had stopped digging when we hit the debris-laden cave floor, where we might have found them had we dug a little deeper. This is all conjecture."

Under this scenario, the collapsed ceiling material would blend in with the rest of the silt, clay, and rock debris in the already debris-laden cave passages and cavers might be unable to discern where the boys' bodies were beneath the cave floor rubble. "Maybe the passage was either closed off by the collapse or the debris covered the bodies, and cavers may have gone right over the top of them," Tripodi said. "It's not unusual to find clay on the floor that's fallen from these ceiling areas. We just assumed that was part of the natural formation of the cave," he added. It is just a theory, one more theory.

Caver Joe Arrigo had his own theory after repeated forays into the subterranean roadcut cave passages. Noting the extensive dynamiting activity that preceded the boys' disappearance, he said, "A lot of us surmised that the boys may have crawled under a 'dynamite bubble.' This a spot where the rock doesn't collapse right away after a detonation because the force of the explosion largely goes upward into the open air, leaving a hollow space beneath the ground just waiting to fully collapse. Then, maybe the boys got in there and messed with the rock ceiling, and tons of it just came down," Arrigo theorized. It would have been an instantaneous end of life for all three boys if they were closely grouped together.

***

During the third week of the search, construction workers in a last-ditch effort removed the face of the Murphy's Cave bluff along Birch street to further expose all openings and any recent collapsed areas that had hampered search efforts. This work involved removing thirty feet of rock and earth across the entire east side of the bluff. It was a final attempt to find any clue to the boys' whereabouts. Three bulldozers from the J.A. Tobin Construction firm removed tons of limestone and shale after dynamiting had loosened up the hillside. Searchers feared recent cave collapses had filled a passage either trapping the boys or crushing them. But, after the additional seearching, no fresh clues emerged.

On Friday, May 26, Speleological Society of America President Bill Karras returned to Hannibal with his team to resume operations. The request had been made by the Hoag family, and this time the SSA team brought a more compact metal detector to use underground.

The heroic cavers tried once again, exploring every available underground avenue throughout the weekend. Another one hundred local volunteers again searched the hills and valleys across the Southside and beyond in one last effort to find the boys.

At 4:30 p.m. on Sunday May 28, the second phase of the search was called off.

At a dinner gathering held to honor the search team, Karras expressed his thanks to the community as well as his regrets. "Hannibal is a town of about 20,000 population, less three. I would like to find those three. And to the people of Hannibal, all we expected was a place to put our sleeping bags and something to eat. We received the best of both, a hotel room and plenty of good food," Karras added. Bob Harrison, Commander of the Mark Twain Emergency Squad commended the cavers and other volunteers for a job well done.

A local fund had raised $26,000 to help organized groups defray the cost of their time and efforts during the eighteen-day search.

The Salvation Army reported its staff had put in 245 hours of service dispensing more than 9,000 cups of coffee, hot chocolate and cold drinks. The searchers had consumed nearly 900 sandwiches, 2,600 donuts and rolls, 488 servings of fried chicken, fish, pork, meatloaf, roast beef, and an abundance of cookies and candy bars. Neighbors and local churches and restaurants had generously donated copious amounts of food and drink, too.

On Wednesday, May 31, State Representative Harold Volkmer introduced House Resolution 231 which was quickly adopted. It reads in part:

> Whereas, On Wednesday, May 10, 1967, Craig Dowell, Joey Hoag, and Billy Hoag, three junior citizens of Hannibal, Missouri, disappeared from that community; and

> Whereas, in spite of the well-organized, massive, and thorough search which followed this tragic mystery, no trace of them has been found.

> Whereas, the search has been officially ended, now, therefore be it resolved by the House of Representatives of the 74th Assembly that this body extends its deepest and sincere sympathy and condolence to Mrs. Helen Dowell, and to Mr. and Mrs. Mike Hoag, and all of Hannibal for the great loss suffered by them.

> Be it further resolved, that the House of Representatives send its expression of gratitude

and appreciation to those who participated, aided
or assisted in the search.

And be it further resolved, that particular mention
be made of those who actually joined in the search,
above or below ground, and upon the river; of
those who provided machinery and equipment,
from the simplest tool to the most complicated
machine; of those who provided and operated
communications equipment which enabled the
participants to be informed of the actions of
others; of those civic and church organizations
which gathered, prepared, and served food and
beverages to the participants; of those who came
great distances to aid in the search because of
their special talents or abilities, or relationship
to the missing boys; of those from far and near
who so generously contributed to the fund of over
$25,000 for the various rescue groups; of the law
enforcement officers who diligently patrolled the
area, directed traffic, and maintained order; and
of the residents and city officials of Hannibal who
kept that city operating throughout this trying and
difficult period."

Tex Yokum, a member of the Mid-Mississippi Valley Grotto
and an officer of the SSA, praised the cavers who had searched so
diligently for so long. "If we are to judge the quality of our future
leaders and officers in the SSA and NSS by the conduct of the
majority of the young people who participated, we have nothing to
worry about," he wrote in his final report to Karras. "At all times,
the reputation of all these young men and women were exposed to
public scrutiny, and we will all benefit by their conduct."

Yokum also expressed frustration about the failed efforts to
track down Joel, Billy and Craig. "To most of us, the search itself
became a constant series of blind leads and empty holes. Even now,

we can't tell where the boys are, but we can tell you where they are not. In the beginning, we felt we had every chance of finding the boys alive. It was very possible that they were lost or trapped, and we worked desperately, knowing what exposure could do to them. This cave system, the 79 cut, as well as [the] Murphy's Cave system, have been examined as thoroughly as any cave I have ever known, not once, but many times. Therefore, we can confidently state that they were not there!"

But there was still no closure to this historic search. Not yet. On Tuesday, June 6, an overflow crowd packed the city hall council chambers, demanding the search continue. The effort was supported by Helen Dowell who had been told by two cavers that the boys may be trapped in an unknown lower level of Murphy's Cave. Mrs. Dowell also asked Governor Warren Hearnes to issue an order to resume the search. "If you will do this for me, then I'll be satisfied," Mrs. Dowell said. She explained that it had been her belief all along that the boys were in Murphy's Cave.

Cavers Lloyd Atwood and Don Vannata claimed they had spent long hours in the cave and believed the boys were buried in a lower level near an entrance. However, they claimed that inadequate air inside the passage had prevented a more thorough search. Most daring of all, Atwood claimed he'd seen shadows that suggested the bodies of the three lost boys were in this lower level. He said he had been hampered from looking more closely due to a large collapse and the dangerous conditions in that area of the cave.

Karras was highly skeptical. Murphy's Cave had been the focus of hundreds of people who spent thousands of hours searching for the boys. In addition, by virtue of the way they are formed, maze caves typically are a complex, horizontal network of interconnecting passages on a single level. Any additional levels would be highly unusual, and would likely have to exist below the water table. "It's possible, but improbable," Karras told city officials.

Deputy State Geologist Jerry Vineyard concurred, noting that Murphy's Cave exists in a narrow band of Louisiana Limestone with only enough room for one level. And, since this cave had more silting than the other maze caves, "it is improbable that any lower levels of the cave exist. Any such passages would in all probability be filled [with silt]."

Karras challenged Atwood to show him where he thought the boys were located. Atwood led Karras through many passages, crossing and recrossing his own path several times.

Finally the men arrived at a spot fifteen feet from where Atwood believed the bodies were located. This location was marked, and the cavers followed the string they had unfurled as they entered.

Once outside, Karras discussed his findings with Tex Yokum and the two cavers reentered the cave. After winding through many passages, the men arrived at the suspect location in fifteen minutes. They found themselves in a small room, essentially a larger intersection of several passages. Working on their knees, the men dug into the cave floor and found nothing. Back at the church, Karras reported his findings to the sheriff at Rescue Control, and a group of curious cavers "walked away in disgust," according to the SSA after-action report. Meanwhile, Atwood reportedly slipped out a back door of the church, according to Karras.

Despite Karras' skepticism, Mark Twain Emergency Squad Vice Commander Bill Bridges thought Atwood's claim was the "only good lead we have had, and I think it should be followed through, regardless of the conflict of individuals."

On June 9, test drillings began as part of the effort to locate a second level in Murphy's Cave. Excitement swept the community, residents hoping the boys' bodies would finally be located after nearly a month.

Caver Joe Tripodi, who was still working in Rescue Control, said there was little opposition to this final effort. "We wanted to do everything we could possibly do to make the families feel better," he explained. "We didn't want anybody thinking that we quit early and hadn't looked everywhere. We were putting our heart and soul into doing everything we could possibly do to find the boys, so the families knew no stone had been left unturned. That was very important to us."

Rescue workers hoped to break into Atwood's supposed lower level, believed to be about eleven feet below a ledge near an entrance to the cave, but there was more to this drilling effort, according to Joe Tripodi in Rescue Control. "One of the things they were looking for were bodily fluids that might be brought up if the boys were in there."

Workers drilled holes nearly thirty feet deep, twenty-four inches apart, across the eastern span of the Murphy's Cave hill, in hopes of finding a clue to the boys' whereabouts.

Mark Twain Emergency Squad workers also dug a hole about seven feet deep using jackhammers, picks and shovels. Then, a large power auger borrowed from Northeast Missouri Electric Power Cooperative was used to drill through the remaining five feet of rock. But no lower level was found at this location. The auger found only mud and gravel down to eighteen feet.

Ironically, Atwood reportedly had chosen to avoid the initial drilling activity. At 2:30 a.m. on June 10, the drilling stopped. The families of the missing boys had remained at the scene for long hours. Backlit by the brilliant rescue lights, their shadows fell across the face of the Murphy's Cave hill, creating a powerful visual statement. Mrs. Dowell, who had requested this final attempt be made, walked to the edge of the deep hole, took a long look into this man-made opening in the earth, and turned slowly away to rejoin family and friends.

No one was more disappointed than the cavers who understood a sad reality about high profile rescue operations; they attract all kinds of people seeking their moment in the limelight. "When you have an event like this, it brings out various types with odd theories," said caver Jerry Vineyard of the Missouri Geological Survey. "They come out of the woodwork with all kinds of conflicting stories that have to be sorted out and explored."

But the drilling crew refused to accept this first defeat. They were back Sunday morning to try again, full of grit and determination. Using pneumatic drills, workers punched into what they believed was a lower passage of Murphy's Cave and quickly enlarged the hole, clearing debris away so cavers could explore this new discovery. Several cavers entered this passage at 8:30 a.m. and carefully explored it, but found only cave debris.

There is no mention of this lower level in Karras' after-action report. In fact, he doesn't even mention Atwood by name, describing what he termed a wild claim made by a man with little or no caving experience who wasted time and endangered cavers.

Perhaps, there's another explanation. Due to recent drilling and extensive excavation along the entire face of the Murphy's Cave bluff, the whole landscape topography had been significantly altered. Had the crew merely opened another hole into a known Murphy's passage, thinking it was a new level? As Karras had stated, maze caves are almost always one level. And none of the other experienced cavers ever suggested Murphy's had a lower level. Regardless, the dedicated searchers had once again come up empty-handed.

It was another heartbreak for Hannibal and signaled the end of the historic search. Karras gathered the caving teams in the Rescue Control operations center at the church. "One of the hardest things we did was to gather in the church and listen as Karras announced that we were quitting," said Hondo caver Brian Borton. "We all went home pretty sad."

As Joe Tripodi helped pack up Rescue Control before driving Karras to the St. Louis Airport, he reflected on the failed search and the burdensome challenge the SSA leader had upon him day after day. "Karras became the Search and Rescue Director because he was an unknown with a title, from out of town. He had political savvy and assumed a job nobody really wanted. God went to a lot of work to put this mystery before Bill Karras."

Chapter 9

Bill Karras, Controversial Caver

"Suddenly, the oppressive blackness of the chamber was broken by the feeble rays of carbide lamps on the ledge high above me. The blinding rays of a flashlight swept over me, and I heard the sound of falling pebbles as someone began to descend to the cave floor. It was Bill Karras, leader of the National Capital Grotto Rescue Team - the nation's crack underground rescue squad. I relaxed. Help had arrived..."

From the October 1965 issue of Popular Science, *How They Rescued Me 200 Feet Underground* by James R. Berry

Most cavers saw Bill Karras as a respected, natural leader dedicated to making caving as safe as possible. After Hannibal, Karras was awarded the State of Missouri's Civil Defense Agency's highest award, "The Distinguished Service Certificate." Agency Director James H. Bash thanked Karras for "...the splendid assistance rendered the city of Hannibal during the tragic search for the missing boys." The award certificate noted his "...untiring and praiseworthy efforts" and said his "...outstanding contribution during the tragic period was in keeping with the highest traditions of public service."

An editorial in the *Kansas City Star* (May 23, 1967) titled *Heartbreak and Gallantry in Hannibal's Hills* lauded the more than one hundred cavers "…who came as far as one thousand miles away to join the fatiguing and often hazardous undertaking." The newspaper editorialist wrote that even the families in their sorrow "…found words of praise for the teams of gallant workers who repeatedly dared the uncharted maze of limestone caverns. Of the man who led the search [Karras], one of the grieving fathers said, 'He couldn't have tried any harder to find our boys if they'd been his own.' That is the ultimate tribute. Though they failed, the searchers gave themselves unselfishly and earned the admiration of all who followed the tragedy—admiration they would gladly have traded for one small cry of a child in the darkness under those Hannibal hills."

Karras had earlier garnered considerable media attention after a high-profile Hinckley, Ohio rescue operation in October 1965. The National Capital Cave Rescue Team responded to an incident in Wildcat Cave in northeastern Ohio. On a cold fall day, fifteen-year-old Morris Baetzold was on a field trip with other children who lived at the Methodist Children's Home in suburban Cleveland. The boy had left the main cave passage during a tour, traversed two big boulders and fell into a narrow crevice, sixty feet from the cave's entrance and thirty-five feet below the surface. Baetzold was stuck fast, head down, face down, with his hands pinned beneath his body, in the forty-five-degree downward slanting passageway which measured a foot wide and three feet high. It was a frightening predicament.

Local rescuers were able to get close to the boy, but not close enough to dislodge him. A teacher from the Methodist Home used a belt to try and snare the boy's feet and pull him out, but the belt broke and Baetzold slipped back again. Rescuers recognized a smaller person was needed to better reach the trapped boy. That's when fifteen-year-old Boy Scout Mike Ulrich from North Royalton, Ohio stepped forward to volunteer.

The heroic five-foot-five, 120-pound sophomore crawled down to Morris, his body coated with water and glycerin to reduce friction and looped straps and a rope around the trapped boy's body. By gently pulling the straps and rope, Baetzold was freed from the crevice that had been his snug prison for twenty-six hours.

Karras, who supervised the operation, had high praise for Ulrich's bravery. When he exited the cave, Karras scooped up Ulrich and carried him to the waiting cameras. "Mike was the real hero of the rescue. The danger to him and the youngster he sought to rescue were paramount at all times," Karras told reporters.

Although Karras' team had arrived sixteen hours into the rescue operation, members were credited by the *Cleveland Plain Dealer* newspaper for their role. "Experience gained in other rescues was applied in finally bringing about the happy outcome." The crevice that had entrapped Baetzold was permanently closed, and the city of Hinckley gave Karras a Certificate of Award in recognition of his efforts on behalf of the community.

Karras had his detractors, too. Some cavers, upset by the lack of success during the Hannibal search and angered by what they described as a "circus-like atmosphere" during the search, saw Karras' desire for media promotion as self-aggrandizing behavior that detracted from the mission.

"Most cavers involved in cave rescues practically abhor the press," explained Jo Schaper, a Missouri speleohistorian. "Often, cavers are too focused on the task at hand to be good PR people and sometimes are too tired to adequately explain themselves. And caves are beyond the ken of most reporters, so incorrect assumptions are often made. Consequently, after several laughable misquotes, most cavers give up talking to members of the press at all and become somewhat secretive."

"Some saw [Karras] as a publicity seeker and cavers typically shun publicity," said caver Bill Walsh. "Karras' people and the Hondo crew from St. Louis wore white coveralls and had a militaristic manner. They did things strictly for the television cameras, wasting precious time. There just seemed to be a lot of caver politics going on. They were all competing to be part of the final glory of the rescue, it seemed," Walsh added.

According to Walsh, many cavers favored Don Black's cave rescue group from Tennessee, seen as solid and responsible. "You have to understand, at the time there were three cave rescue organizations, Karras' SSA, the Hondo Underground Rescue Team in St. Louis, and Don Black's cave rescue unit of the Chattanooga-Hamilton County Rescue Service," Walsh explained. The widely respected Tennessee cave rescue group was formed in the early 1960s to provide cave search and rescue services across the southeastern United States.

Bill Karras seemed to be driven by a dual motivation—find and extricate the missing, injured or trapped persons alive and, in the process, work with the media to keep the public informed and to heighten awareness of the need for and the importance of cave rescue services. Although skilled and well-intentioned, Karras didn't always wear both hats well.

***

In 1963, Karras created the Washington DC area National Capital Cave Rescue Team (NATCAP), pulling members from the Virginia Region VAR grotto, where he had served as a vice-chairman. The NATCAP group acquired a Cadillac which was modified into an ambulance to haul equipment and, if necessary, a victim to the hospital.

Karras' creation of the rescue group came after his involvement in a daring mountaineering accident while training. Karras and several caving colleagues were practicing climbing skills on a nine hundred-foot-high column of rocky terrain in West Virginia when one of the men suffered a crushed leg in a landslide of basketball-sized rocks. Bleeding profusely from a torn artery, the man was rescued by his clear-headed friends who staunched the bleeding, expertly lowered him down a four hundred-foot cliff, and raced him to the hospital for treatment.

"Coming home, we asked ourselves what would happen in an *underground* accident," Karras explained. "Underground exploring is a very specialized form of caving, yet there was no organized rescue team anywhere. We decided on the spot to form one," he told a reporter for *Popular Science* magazine.

Three years later, the National Capital Rescue Team would

evolve into Karras' vision for a larger, national organization during an era when many organizations felt the turmoil sweeping the country as a generation rebelled against authority and regulatory intrusion.

William Karras, founder and director of the Speleological Society of America (SSA), was one of the nation's most experienced cave rescue specialists during the 1960s, but his authoritarian style and a desire for publicity irritated many cavers. Photo courtesy Quincy Herald-Whig.

In launching his own national cave organization, the Speleological Society of America (SSA), Karras was taking on the well-established, credible National Speleological Society (NSS). Since its creation in 1941, the prestigious NSS had consisted of skilled, science-minded individuals who greatly desired the NSS' scientific structure and agenda. However, as caving captured the imagination of a new generation, the NSS felt pressure from these weekend sports cavers. These men and women were often more interested in pursuing their own fun adventures rather than attending speleological seminars on topics like hydrology, biology and geology.

Karras' experience exemplified the struggles within the NSS and across the caving communities in the US. His formation of the SSA as an alternative organization created tension in the caving community. It meant a potential loss of revenue and members for the NSS as both national caving organizations elbowed for the spotlight.

Garland "Gary" Black III, now seventy-three and a resident of suburban Washington, DC, was a member of Karras' rescue team beginning in late 1965. Black found Karras demanding but highly committed to safe caving. "He was a good teacher and a father figure for many of the young men. He was loud and forceful, always in charge, some might say to a fault. He could be very demanding. He *told* us, he didn't *ask*. It wasn't mean-spirited, he just wanted a better caving organization for all concerned."

"The NSS did not support Bill's vision to have the SSA handle cave search and rescue cases, but we wanted a cave rescue infrastructure. The NSS published a great journal, but it only carried articles by scientists in specialties like geology and hydrology. We wanted a voice to reach all cavers about important cave safety and search and rescue topics," Black explained.

Karras was driven to create an infrastructure to support cave search and rescue. Cavers frequently visited Karras' seven-hundred-acre farm he leased near Winchester, Virginia. After his first marriage had failed, Karras and his second wife, Janelle, decided to move to the country.

"We'd often go to his farm on the weekends to train," Black said. "We were also slave labor, helping him feed cattle and renovate a house for a poor family. We set up a training program and brought in Red Cross instructors who certified us in first aid. It was good basic training that helped all of us."

Karras often took the team caving in West Virginia. "We explored lots of limestone caves. Some were just tunnels, and others were breakdown caves with lots of debris down. It was great experience for all of us," Black explained. "Bill was very detailed about what he wanted. He insisted on safety for everyone, so we needed training to recover people from caves. The SSA was made up of very dedicated cavers who benefited from his strong training and educational program."

Missouri speleologist Jerry Vineyard was an NSS director in the early 1960s and served as editor of the *NSS Bulletin* newsletter. He recalled the SSA-NSS clash clearly as a conflict over priorities. "Along comes Bill Karras who felt like cavers ought to take care of their own, and there ought to be a highly trained professional national cave rescue outfit that could mobilize in minutes and fly off anywhere in the country and rescue folks. But his message and approach didn't sell very well in the NSS hierarchy at the time. They pretty much blew him off. So he and some other people went their own way with their own organization, the SSA," Vineyard said.

Karras was heavily promoting a search and rescue role as the sport of caving grew in popularity. When life-threatening cave rescue crises developed, Karras often was found at the center of the operations. "Caving isn't a dangerous sport," Karras told an interviewer, "but it's growing fast, and many people just don't take time to learn the rules." Karras set out to make sports caving a safe avocation so spelunkers had the proper training, equipment and exhibited good judgment in karst environments.

St. Louis caver Conway Christensen, who had extensive experience caving in New Mexico, Texas, Virginia, and Missouri, first met Bill Karras in April 1965 when their respective teams responded to a cave rescue incident in Fiftysix, Arkansas. Four men had entered a remote Ozark mountain cave, despite a forecast of heavy rain. While they were underground, torrential rain fell, causing the water level in the cave to rise quickly, trapping the men for two days deep inside Rowland Cave. "That case involved using divers to breach the dark, swirling water in order to get into the cave," Christensen explained.

Air Force II flew Karras and his team to Arkansas, according to Garland Black, a Karras team member. Enroute, the men received maps of the cave via an onboard fax machine that far surpassed consumer technology at the time. Once there, Black explained, "Our divers laid a cable into the cave so the men could follow it out. We brought in scuba gear and gave them quick instruction in its use, and then brought them out one at a time. It was a slow, tedious job in zero visibility and underwater. The last guy was almost out of air by the time we got him out."

While the four men were successfully rescued, a team diver got disoriented in the murky water, panicked and suffered a heart attack in the tight confines of the cave. "He was a deep-sea diving instructor for the US Navy," Christensen explained. "Those kinds of incidents really hurt—when you successfully retrieve those who were trapped due to their own foolish behavior only to have an injury or death to a rescuer who would not have been there normally," Christensen lamented.

The National Capital Rescue Squad consisted of two squads of six members each. Three members held certifications as expert scuba divers trained in underwater rescue operations. The team members regularly drilled in advanced first aid and rescue techniques, and their gear always remained packed and ready should an emergency arise. As was the case in Hannibal, Karras tapped contacts at the Pentagon to use military aircraft to quickly ferry his rescue team to cave emergencies across the nation.

The NATCAP team's first high profile test occurred on the weekend of February 13, 1965 when twenty-three-year-old caver James Mitchell and two friends were exploring the Schroeder's Pants Cave near Dolgeville, New York. The three had lowered themselves into the cave Saturday morning and crawled seventy-five feet through wet and muddy passages, some of them very tight squeezes, until they arrived in a small room. The trio peered down into a sixty-foot-deep cavern which had an icy stream cascading into the opening. Mitchell, a brilliant student at the Massachusetts Institute of Technology working on the Gemini Space Project, erected an iron tripod over the breach and affixed a rope, letting the other end fall into the cavern. Then, using Prusix slings for stirrups, he lowered himself twenty feet to a jutting ledge.

On the way back up, Mitchell got stuck in the worst possible spot. Icy, thirty-four-degree water poured over him at a rate of eight to ten gallons per minute. His hands quickly grew numb, his carbide light extinguished, and Mitchell found himself suspended eight feet from the top of the pit. All efforts by his friends to pull him up failed. One of his companions raced to a nearby farmhouse to seek help.

After the Dolgeville Fire Department personnel responded and failed to retrieve Mitchell, Karras was notified and the National Capital Rescue Team flew to a military base in Rome, NY and helicoptered to Dolgeville, arriving on scene before dawn Sunday.

Karras, thirty-nine, allowed only his team members into the cave, insisting that for safety purposes he, rather than a local physician, would use an electronic stethoscope to check Mitchell's condition.

"Mitchell was snow white when we saw him, and we knew he couldn't aid us," Karras said. "The dirty part of this thing is he didn't get hurt, just cold." The rescuers again tried to raise Mitchell without success. Then, Karras told authorities his team had lowered Mitchell's body forty-five feet to the cave floor and followed him down. By 8:30 p.m. Sunday, Karras told state police he had not detected any signs of life and would seal the corpse in a body bag.

Losing a trapped spelunker stung; there would be no heroic rescue, only a body recovery now lay ahead, and a difficult one, too. Since Mitchell's body could not be brought up through the narrow passage from which he'd descended, a drilling apparatus was set up to drill into the pit from the surface.

Two of Karras' men were preparing to drop into the pit to retrieve the victim's belongings, make formal identification, and body bag the remains when a series of low-pitched rumbles echoed through the cave. Believing it was the drilling mechanism on the surface, a caver called up to Karras to have the machinery turned off.

Karras saw that the drilling equipment was not operating so quickly yelled, "Tell them to get the hell out of there! The cave's starting to collapse!" Karras' two team members narrowly escaped, sustaining cuts and abrasions as debris tumbled into the cave passage. "A minute later," Karras remarked, "and we'd have had three dead men in that cave."

Worried about additional cave-ins, the state approved Karras' recommendation to dynamite the cave entrance to close it with Mitchell's body still inside. Not only had Karras' team failed to rescue Mitchell, the cavers were unable to even recover his body.

Karras termed the five-day rescue attempt as the "toughest assignment" he'd encountered in more than two decades of cave exploration. While in the area, Karras spoke to the student body at Dolgeville Central School telling the youngsters to avoid caves so he would not have to return in the future to recover them. A school official wrote Karras thanking him for his selflessness in coming to the aid of the trapped caver:

> "You attacked relentlessly and at great personal risk, a task of unimaginable difficulty and strengthened us by your efforts. You held all who worked in the rescue to the highest professional standards. Your efforts will long serve as a standard of achievement for those who have had the privilege of knowing you."

> Very truly yours,
> Rodney W. Pierce, Director of Guidance

In the summer of 1965 two cavers, Jim Crane and Duane Lyon, were exploring near the Schroeder's Pants Cave when they heard rocks falling and found the cave open. "It was eerie," Crane would later say, "almost like Mitchell's ghost was calling us to enter or telling us it was okay to be there."

Inside, the men found no indication of a major collapse, only evidence that debris had fallen from the ceiling during the earlier drilling. Mitchell's body, they reported, was found doubled over with debris covering the top of his body. They said the rope that had held Mitchell appeared to have been cut. They found an unused body bag near the body. In their view, Karras probably could have retrieved Mitchell's body.

Mitchell's body was finally recovered in 2006 thanks to efforts put into motion by Christian Lyon, a Dolgeville native whose grandfather George Lyon had discovered the Schroeder's Pants Cave in 1947. Lyon convinced Doug Bradford, an original member of the National Capital Rescue Team, to assist with recovery of Mitchell's remains. This time, they were able to accomplish what the Karras team had been unable to do in 1965. They brought Mitchell's remains to the surface for his family to lay to rest. The family spread some of Mitchell's cremains near the cave and the remainder in a pond on family property back in Ohio.

The caving community would remember that not everyone walked away alive from a Karras operation. And sometimes, even a body was left behind.

***

Speleological Society of America founder Bill Karras is interviewed by a reporter for the next day's front page story. Photo courtesy Hannibal Courier-Post.

On October 29, 1966, after years of planning, Karras formally established the Speleological Society of America (SSA), just eight months before the team would be called to Hannibal. In his organizational newsletter, *SSA Speleologist*, Karras wrote:

> Even the most casual explorer will benefit, however brief his contact with the Society or its members. The goodwill and feeling for safety among fellow cavers will instill in him the desire for team spirit and companionship. Caving is a new science and a new art, and a lot is yet to be learned about it.

And in another newsletter issue, Karras wrote, "As with any new organization, there are growing pains. We are being scrutinized and criticized, but such is to be expected." Those were prescient words from the man who would soon be in the spotlight as Hannibal's terrible human drama played out on the national stage.

In one issue of *SSA Speleologist*, member Bob West noted the important rescue role the SSA would serve nationally. "In hundreds of caves in this country, a broken hand or leg could mean the difference between life and death for the victim. The unwise unskilled novice opens the door to a serious accident or even death," he penned. "Caving... is an exciting and rewarding activity when it is properly tempered by good training and common sense. However, in the past year the number of accidents has increased below the surface of the ground. In many of these cases, the injured person lay in pain while a companion went for help. And when help came, their lack of cave technique in many instances stopped the rescue until others were summoned who were properly trained. This procedure required and wasted valuable hours," West concluded.

Conway Christensen, writing in his own grotto's newsletter, noted another role for the SSA—the promotion of cave conservation. "Speleology is rapidly coming to the foreground with the interest in wild caving growing by leaps and bounds. Nearly every high school and college in a caving area has a group of spelunkers. Education has become of prime concern to us in the society in order to prevent vandalism and thereby destruction of one of the world's most unusual and unknown wildernesses."

Karras' considerable skills as a promoter had already been employed in advance of the SSA's formation. A year earlier, the October 1965 issue of *Popular Science* magazine hit newsstands with the high-profile feature story about Karras, his cave rescue team, and the growing need for cave search and rescue expertise. In the article, *How They Rescued Me 200 Feet Underground,* writer James R. Berry assumed the role of injured victim in a simulated cave rescue exercise, with Karras and his team cast as the heroes.

> A musty smell of wet clay permeated the huge cave chamber, and from one of dozens of tiny side passages a slow, methodical drip of water seemed to ring through the stillness like the blows of a hammer. The most surprising thing, though, was the cold. Before my 'fall' down the 40-foot-high underground cliff, I had been warm from crawling down the cave's narrow passages and climbing through its rooms. Now, lying quietly on the damp floor at the cliff's bottom, my breath steamed and a chill from the floor penetrated my clothes. Suddenly, the oppressive blackness of the chamber was broken by the feeble rays of carbide lamps on the ledge high above me. The blinding rays of a flashlight swept over me, and I heard the sound of falling pebbles as someone began to descend to the cave floor. It was Bill Karras, leader of the National Capital Grotto Rescue Team - the nation's crack underground rescue squad. I relaxed. Help had arrived...

Later, a January 9, 1966 feature story in the *Baltimore Sun,* credited Karras and his team with saving more than forty lives. A local caving club official who read the story questioned the figure and invited Karras to explain his numbers. Further investigation found that the figure included National Capital Rescue Squad responses to automobile accidents, mock rescues, lost hikers, and lost cavers who found their way out before Karras had even been on the scene.

So Karras' public relations fell short of reality in the minds of many cavers. The caving community had plenty to say after witnessing Karras' actions at Hannibal and elsewhere. In an editorial in a Virginia Region (VAR) grotto newsletter, a member wrote:

> Bill moved into D.C.-area caving like a tornado, full of cave facts, claims of past accomplishments and a desire for power and attention. He soon made himself known to all the "in" people in the D.C. area, the VAR, and the NSS. People who thought he was a phony were few; those who did believe him defended him angrily.

But, once again, we see evidence of the disdain for Karras' personality traits that were an anathema to cavers who prefer to maintain a low profile with no media attention to distract them during a search and rescue operation. Cavers recognize that caves are beautiful, unique and fragile environments, eons in the making, and must be protected from overuse and misuse by the untrained.

> Karras made a lot of mistakes; he tried to set himself up as the national cave rescuer; he was driven by a need for attention, power and glory.

But the VAR writer acknowledged that Karras, however painfully, did motivate the caving community to become better prepared to handle cave rescues.

> Looking back, we know that Bill's efforts to provide cave rescue personnel and equipment eventually spurred persons to form [search and rescue] groups...and encouraged [grottos] to set up first aid courses for members and to train their members in more responsible caving techniques, as well as more effective rescue techniques.

Many cavers have spent time, money and energy certifying themselves as EMTs in order to be better prepared for any situation.

The *Baltimore Grotto*, in its May 1967 newsletter, addressed its members' concerns about Karras' approach on the timely subject of cave rescue.

> The recent events in Hannibal, Missouri, in which three young boys disappeared, apparently in a cave, and the rapid arrival on the scene of a discredited former member of the NSS, dramatically point out the necessity for an efficient, effective rescue service well known to local police and Civil Defense workers. With the increasing popularity of caving and rock climbing and the attendant appearance of many untrained people in the caves and hills, it is only a matter of time before there is a serious accident involving loss of life and much undesirable publicity of such a nature that many caves and rock climbing areas will be closed forever. It would only take one inept "rescue" and resulting publicity to destroy what we all have worked and played at.

Search participant Wayne Finch, from the Middle Mississippi Valley Grotto, had arrived in Hannibal two days into the search operation. He found tensions already high between Karras and many cavers. Finch shared his thoughts in an article titled *Fiasco in Hannibal*, published in the grotto's June 1967 newsletter *The Underground*:

> I had been previously told that I shouldn't form an opinion about Karras until I met the man and talked to him. After I met the man and talked to him, and saw him in action, my opinion did change. It was lowered considerably. I saw nothing but a flamboyant, egotistic, publicity seeking glory

hunter... interested only in glorifying the image of Bill Karras.

The final straw was when I was standing with a group of ten or twelve people and Karras was instructing a man to get a boat and check some of the islands in the river. He told the man, 'If you find those little SOBs, don't tell anyone. Not the police or the parents. Let me know and I'll come and get them and make the announcement.' That was it. I walked away, sickened. This whole rescue operation left me with a bad taste in my mouth. In my own mind, I was 100 percent certain that the boys were not in the Lover's Leap area, so I felt no discredit in leaving... Karras is not qualified to lead a trip into a cave, much less a rescue operation.

John Hempel, a geological consultant and member of the Eastern Cave Rescue Commission, kept his comments succinct: "Karras was a glory hound who set caving back ten years."

The national caving community was prompt to address what was widely perceived as Karras' unpopular cave search practices. Later in 1967, after the Hannibal operation, Don Black, a leader of the respected Chattanooga-Hamilton County Rescue Service in cave-rich Tennessee, was appointed National Cave Rescue Coordinator for the National Speleological Society. In a letter to all US grottos, Black laid out his strategic vision, as detailed in the November 1967 issue of the *Baltimore Grotto* newsletter:

...experiences of recent months have emphasized the need for national coordination, and an attempt should be made to bring some semblance of order to the rather chaotic condition which exists. This is not a "one man show" and does not call for someone to dash madly by jet all over the country whenever the opportunity for publicity appears. It is rather my intention to enlist the aid of Regional Rescue Directors. These men know the caves in their areas, and they know and are known by the cavers they will be supervising under emergency conditions.

In other words, keep a rescue as local as possible, the opposite of the national rescue approach Karras had advocated. Black called for nominations for several Regional Officers positions, noting these individuals must be qualified, trusted and capable. Black wrote:

These men should be expert in all phases of cave exploration, both horizontal and vertical, be skilled in applicable first aid techniques, and have the qualities of leadership that will enable them to direct an emergency situation in the field with a minimum of confusion and a maximum of safety and efficiency.

The 1967 issue of the National Speleological Society's *American Caving Accidents* publication details a short summary of the Hannibal search, ending with this:

A massive search of all caves in the area, by experienced cave explorers, under the direction of William Karras, turned up no trace of the missing boys. Analysis: The consensus is that, with a high probability, the three boys were lost in a cave - but could not be found despite the effort expended. If true, this stands as unique in cave rescue efforts, but not at all unusual in the annals of mountaineering accidents.

In a special NSS publication, *Caving in America: The story of the National Speleological Society 1941-1991*, editors noted the Karras-led Schroeder's Pants rescue attempt in Dolgeville, New York, surrounded by publicity but ending in failure, hurt caving's image during the 1960s. And citing the Hannibal search, the article's writers noted:

Critics of the rescue effort were outspoken and as a result, some reputations were ruined during the name-calling period. It impacted not only the national cave rescue groups but affected all cave rescue teams. As a result many cavers came to distrust "rescue heroes" glorified in news articles and national rescue teams soon came under fire. Many quit rescue entirely. A slowing of cave rescue preparedness ensued and lasted for about 10 years.

Pennsylvania-based Speleohistorian Jack Speece has spent years studying William G. Karras and the cave rescue operations he led. At a 2008 NSS convention in Lake City, Florida, Speece presented a paper entitled *William Karras and the Speleological Society of America.*

William Karras became quite a central figure between 1965 and 1967 due to his highly publicized rescue attempts.... His aggressive style, along with an eye for publicity and a knack for showmanship, rankled many. But in a crisis he took control and got results. Many were concerned about the impressions and standards that Karras imposed on young novice cavers. Although Bill's efforts to become a national cave rescue hero were not appreciated by the general caving population, he did show the need to have trained personnel and equipment. This spurred grottos and regions to set up first aid courses, technique classes and rescue sessions. Rescue teams were soon organized and properly trained throughout the country.

One of Karras' own teammates recognized the controversial caver's nature. "When I first met Karras, he was already a controversial figure in caving circles. His aggressive style, along with an eye for publicity and a knack for showmanship, rankled many," Speece related in his 2008 NSS Convention presentation.

Speece presented another paper on Karras' role in the 1965 Schroeder's Pants Cave rescue debacle at the June 2017 NSS convention held in New Mexico. Speece wrote:

> Cavers... have prided themselves in recovering their lost companions at almost any cost....The decision to abandon the rescue efforts at Dolgeville (NY) brought about some serious [disagreements] between the established NSS cavers of the area and the non-affiliated rescue group lead by Karras... Karras would later be banned from the NSS and considered to be a "glory seeker" by most members.

Speece wrote that the lessons learned from the flawed 1960s cave rescue operations motivated the caving community to shun Karras' nationalistic model for cave rescue in favor of a more regional approach, utilizing trained cavers familiar with their own regions' caves, geology, and emergency services agencies.

> The National Capital Rescue Squad (NATCAP) was the first formal effort of its kind. They were young, inexperienced, and had to improvise their techniques and equipment. An auxiliary team from Hondo Grotto (HURT) was also formed in Missouri. These Speleological Society of America groups would ...make headlines [that]... brought about much criticism.

> Mitchell's death and several others shortly afterwards...made the caving community realize that they needed to have a proper organization and response for underground emergencies. This led to the formation of the *National Cave Rescue Commission* with teams around the country. It took about ten years years to properly prepare

rescue guidelines, overcome critics that felt rescue leaders were all egotists, and gain the public's respect. Today, these organized and well trained organizations are ready, willing and able to respond to any emergency.

Brian Borton, a teenage member of the St. Louis-based Hondo Underground Rescue Team in 1967, later spent decades exploring some of the world's largest caverns. Borton also participated in the elaborate 1991 rescue of caver Emily Davis who broke her leg while exploring Lechuguilla Cave in New Mexico, the third longest cave in the US with nearly 140 miles of passages. Miles from the surface, Davis was successfully extricated. Borton, now a St. Louis pilot, understands the challenges of Karras' leadership role during the historic search. "Hannibal was a small community getting national attention. The press was inundating us, hanging around the operations center at the church. Karras was constantly approached by the media, by everyone. He took on a big task and was sweating bullets when the boys weren't turning up. He was the media guy, and Incident Command Training teaches that you need a media guy. A lot of people didn't deal well with that, but it was necessary," Borton said. "Put yourself in Bill's place. We didn't have much positive to report during that search," Borton explained. "We were all trying to do the best job we could. We did everything in our power to find the boys. No one shirked their responsibility."

Caver Jim Arrigo saw both sides of Karras' complex nature. "Person to person he was all right, but he had this grandiose personality and wanted to be in charge of everything. Yes, he knew a lot about cave rescue but liked to be in the limelight, too," Arrigo explained. "He had a quirk about wanting to soak up all the glory. Having said that, I don't know if there could have been anyone better to head up the search. The media needed someone to talk to, and Karras was always willing. He was in charge so I followed him. It was such an emergency, you had to put aside personality and politics."

It's striking that one individual could draw so many strong, widely divergent opinions. The public, government agencies, and many cavers respected Karras as a knowledgeable cave search and rescue specialist. Yet, other cavers held him in deep disregard and contempt. It is easy to understand how turf battles could erupt. Consider the typical scenario: Karras, the national expert, flying in on Air Force II and taking over operations from local or regional cavers who likely knew the targeted cave, its geology, and local emergency response authorities better than most. Perhaps egos were bruised, as the flamboyant Karras claimed the limelight, but it's clear that cavers have in mind the best interest of the injured, trapped or missing during these tense, high profile operations. And anything beyond the focused task of finding the victim(s) is often seen by many cavers as unhelpful distraction.

Chapter 10

Bodies in the Basement?

On Mother's Day, May 10, 1992, Helen Hoag, the only surviving parent, dressed in her Sunday best, attended a memorial service held atop Lover's Leap. This was the twenty-fifth anniversary of the boys' disappearance, and 150 family members, friends and local residents had made a solemn pilgrimage to this high overlook for the dedication of a gray granite memorial marker to Joel, Billy and Craig.

Hannibal resident Gary Rush, who had attended school with Joel Hoag and Craig Dowell, parked his car along busy Highway 79 and made the steep walk up the twisting narrow road to the top of the Leap. "Tim Hoag met me at the bottom, and he was very appreciative of my coming. I know it meant a lot to him and the other family members to have such a good turnout."

Speaking to the crowd, Helen Hoag dabbed her eyes as she looked out across the quiet mass of friends. "This memorial has been needed for a long time, it makes it more final," she told them. The lengthy search, at a cost of more than $1.5 million, had been a devastating life-changing event, with a priceless human toll, for the families and the residents in the region.

Helen's oldest son, Fred, remembered his beloved brothers as inquisitive, natural boys. "Joey was the scientist of the family. He had a telescope and studied the stars. He questioned everything.

Billy was like his shadow. He'd go along with anything just to have a good time. He was a happy-go-lucky kid," Fred said as sobs could be heard through the crowd. "This memorial is as much for the community as anything. I guess you could say the three boys were the sons of the city."

Bill Bridges, the former vice chairman of the Mark Twain Emergency Squad, the first responders to the scene on May 10, 1967, said his men could not have handled the enormous task facing them alone. "Miraculously, everyone pitched in," he said as he expressed gratitude to the hundreds of dedicated, knowledgeable cavers and other personnel who had come from throughout the nation to find Hannibal's lost boys.

Hannibal Mayor John Yancey had designated this Sunday *A Day of Remembrance*, recalling the many sleepless nights he too had spent thinking about the lost children twenty-five years earlier.

State Representative Steve Carroll read a Missouri House resolution honoring the efforts of the rescue volunteers and local service organizations that aided during the search. He extended the state's heartfelt sympathies to the Hoag and Dowell families and gave each family member a copy of the resolution.

Bill Dean, a stepbrother of Craig Dowell, extended his thanks and gratitude to those who helped in the search and funded the memorial. Marty Hodges, a good friend of Fred Hoag, and the primary organizer of the event, unveiled the memorial stone, its message inscribed on a bronze plaque:

Craig Dowell   Joey Hoag   Billy Hoag

On May 10, 1967, three adventurous boys explored these hills in the footprints of Huckleberry Finn and Tom Sawyer only to never be seen again. Craig, Joey, and Billy will be remembered by rescue teams who came from coast to coast to solve the disappearance. These boys are dearly missed and loved by their families and friends, but will never be forgotten by all. This historical monument also reflects the love of the community and a nation who helped in the search.

The Memorial stone was moved to a more visible location on Lover's Leap in the spring of 2017.

Hoag family friend Marty Hodges, kneeling, and Fred Hoag at the memorial marker located on Lover's Leap. Photo courtesy Hannibal Courier-Post.

Gary Rush, now a bailiff for Marion County Courts, stepped up to see the memorial, a ritual he would repeat many times in coming years, always quietly asking the same question, "Where did you go, guys?" For Rush, the memorial service did not have the finality of the grave. "I see it as more of a salute to the lives of three boys we were blessed to have known during childhood while growing up in our own little version of Mayberry," Rush explained.

Conway Christensen, who'd led the St. Louis-based Hondo Underground Rescue Team in 1967, was also present for the dedication. As he stepped forward and read the plaque, he knew its message would be seen in the years ahead by many thousands of tourists who would come to this scenic high point and take in the dramatic sweep of historic Hannibal and the Mississippi River. The story of the lost boys, he thought, and those who searched for them, would not be forgotten.

"Afterwards, we had a gathering and shared a meal at the Hoag house," Christensen said. "I visited with Mrs. Hoag who expressed her deep appreciation for everything that had been done to try to find the three boys. I still think about it from time to time. It's just such a mystery."

Pastors Tim Goodman and Larry Veatch had offered prayers of dedication, healing and peace for the surviving family members and friends. Members of the Northeast Missouri Area Vietnam Veterans organization placed a wreath at the memorial. It was a sacred moment in a high place in America's Hometown. And the solemn memorial ceremony was a balm for the mourning that had continued over many years in the absence of three bodies not yet able to be laid to rest.

Incredibly, another chapter of this sad story would soon be written. In April 1996, an ugly rumor reopened the emotional wound left from the lost boys' tragedy and brought the story back into the headlines for another generation. The rumor was serious enough to get police attention. "If there's any possibility that we could come to closure on this case, we'd like to do anything we could," Hannibal Police Lt. Joey Runyon told a reporter for the *Quincy Herald-Whig*. "Right now, we have no evidence whatsoever. All we're doing is entertaining a hypothesis from a private individual," the officer added.

This latest drama began November 15, 1995 when retired Hannibal Police Department Detective Charles Webster received a phone call from a man who identified himself as Carl Michael Bailey, a Kirksville resident. Webster's report indicated that Bailey had lived in Hannibal and "was a boy scout when the boys was [sic] lost in the cave, and he worked helping at the caves" during the search.

According to Webster, Bailey, a community leader who managed a fast food restaurant, had heard a rumor that allegedly originated with a relative of Craig Dowell. Bailey said he was coming forward only in the interest of finding the truth in the high-profile case.

The rumor was shocking, as detailed in the official Hannibal Police report, penned by Lt. Joe Hunold, dated November 16, 1995:

> ...the [Hoag] father had killed the three kids, and buried them in the basement of the residence they were living at. The reason for this was that the mother and father were going to go shopping, and told the kids to stay out of the caves. When they parents left, the kids headed towards the caves. When the parents returned, the father was extremely upset and began to whip the boys. He apparently beat the kids to death, and buried them in the basement of 621 Fulton.

Playing citizen detective, Bailey advised police he'd researched the Hannibal incident and found that, as detailed in the police report, "all the different ways of what could have happened had been explored but one. He advised that the [Hoag] family was never interviewed or questioned. The residence was never searched. I asked this of Capt. Webster, and he concurred. Webster advised that they had no reason not to believe the Hoags story."

For that matter, the Dowell house and property had not been searched either.

Based only on hearsay, police did not reopen the investigation, but investigators did speak with the new owners of the house to ascertain the conditions in the basement when they'd purchased the property. The owners, who did not wish to be identified, were concerned about any excavation being done, not knowing who would bear the cost and what damage any digging might inflict on the house. The property owner, tired of seeing the parade of curiosity seekers driving by, told police the basement was intact and ended the inquiry. "There certainly are no bones in our basement, and I feel sorry for the family," said one of the owners.

Lynnie Hoag Pedigo said that when her parents moved out of the house years earlier, the basement was undisturbed. The lower level was comprised of three rooms, one of which housed a large gas furnace common in older homes in the era. The basement rooms had concrete floors, but a dirt portion extended under the front porch which was supported by footings set deep in the ground. This earthen floor, she said, had always remained dry, hard packed and showed no evidence of having ever been disturbed.

The dark rumor was untrue, but it left another painful mark on the Hoag family psyche. "We'd all heard that terrible gossip. Daddy never whipped or beat us," Lynnie said. "There were so many cruel things said. You'd think people had better things to do."

Fred Hoag said the rumor stirred up a lot of sad memories that were very upsetting to the families and area residents who grieve the lost boys. "There's never been anything that would prove something other than a disappearance, a mystery. God only knows, and until we get there, we'll never know."

Police Close Investigation into Boys' Disappearance
By Margie Clark, Courier Post Staff Writer
April 25, 1996

The Hannibal Police Department's most recent investigation of the unsolved 1967 disappearance of three Hannibal boys has ended.

On May 10, 1967, Billy Hoag, 10, Joey Hoag, 13 and Craig Dowell, 14, were last seen entering a cave on Hannibal's Southside, and were never seen again.

After an intensive search for 2 1/2 weeks, the case was abandoned, with no new leads.

Recent rumors and police calls to the police department, indicating the boys might have been murdered, promoted an investigation last week that has led to nothing specific.

Contact with family members and present property owners has been completed according to Lt. Joey Runyon of the Hannibal police department. "We checked to see if we could access the property, so tests could be done," said Runyon. "The property owners were concerned with the possibility that excavation might have to be done, and not knowing who would be responsible for paying for the repair work."

The current owners of the former Hoag property on Hannibal's Southside, says the traffic jam caused by curiosity seekers in the alley has died down. As far as the owners are concerned the investigation and prying into their privacy is over.

They are concerned that the basement of their house could have been destroyed for no reason. Mike Bailey of Kirksville, a private citizen who was pursuing the investigation, said anything he has to say on the subject makes it seem self-serving. He insists that is not the case.

"My heart aches for everyone who is a victim of this horrible story, and they should be given the best information as to what led to this," said Bailey. "If the police department feels it is proper to end the investigation, then I support them 100 percent. If anyone has any new information that would help in this case, I would like for them to turn it over to the proper authorities."

According to Runyon, nothing more can be done unless new information surfaces. "Any good information given, or probable cause, we would definitely pursue, but at this point speculation cannot get a search warrant issued," he said.

Mary Jo Deney Powell, the former Hoag neighbor who knew the family well, expressed her frustration about the 'bodies in the basement' rumor in a *Letter to the Editor* published April 26, 1996 in the Hannibal Courier-Post. She chided the rumor mill for coming up with "ugly rumors and gossip that only slanders the Hoag name. It is my opinion the Hoags have had their share of hurts and sorrows for a lifetime."

She closed with this:

To the Hoag family who are left, I offer my sincere sympathy for the renewed pain you must feel because I do, and that twenty-nine years ago, I couldn't get anyone to listen to our story that was told to us by Billy. I tried, but no one would listen. I just never got loud enough, I guess. I'm sorry.

Powell had never truly known whether cave rescue personnel explored the area described by Billy the day before the boys disappeared. Certainly, the roadcut was a central focus, but had the crews dug far enough into the roadcut hill itself to find the area Billy had so excitedly described to Mrs. Powell? The record is unclear, but it would be difficult to believe Billy's new spot escaped the scrutiny of so many cavers who so intensely focused their attention on a relatively small area of the Highway 79 roadbed.

The lost boy's parents, Helen and Mike Hoag and Helen Dowell, were deceased when the basement rumor hit the news, so they were spared of more earthly pain. The surviving Hoag and Dowell family members must have quietly wondered if this tragic story would ever end so they could find some peace.

Chapter 11

Underground Again, Renewed Hope

Ten years passed before another development again shook the Hannibal community, as another generation was introduced to the lost boys' story in a dramatic reprise of what had unfolded in 1967. This tragic story refused to stay buried in history.

In April 2006, construction was underway for a new Stowell Elementary School to replace the old, red brick school attended by generations of Southsiders as far back as 1924. The school construction project, just west of Highway 79, required demolition of the Southside Christian Church, the parsonage, and several homes along Fulton and Union streets, including the Hoag family homestead.

Once the big excavators began tearing away brick, lumber, rubble and earth, construction workers once again exposed a portion of the underground cave network beneath Fulton Avenue and the area where the street would eventually be rerouted as part of the new school construction project. Fern Martin, Pastor Elba Martin's wife, had long ago noticed the parsonage's living room was cooler and sometimes smelled musty. It all made sense now. There was, indeed, a cave beneath the house.

It was exciting news. Instantly, the story went viral as local residents saw this as another opportunity to find the lost boys who had gone missing thirty-nine years earlier. "There is a history here," said Missouri Department of Transportation (MODOT) Northeast District Engineer Kirk Juranas. "There were three children that lived very close to this site. We know there is a local concern about those kids. We just need to be open and honest and share all the information we have so people can trust we are doing the right thing."

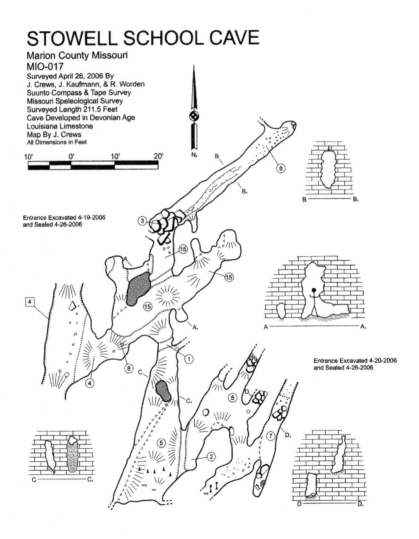

STOWELL SCHOOL CAVE

Marion County Missouri
MIO-017
Surveyed April 26, 2006 By
J. Crews, J. Kaufmann, & R. Worden
Suunto Compass & Tape Survey
Missouri Speleological Survey
Surveyed Length 211.5 Feet
Cave Developed in Devonian Age
Louisiana Limestone
Map By J. Crews
All Dimensions in Feet

Map of Stowell Cave, compiled by J. Crews, Missouri Speleological Survey. Surveyed by J. Crews, J. Kaufmann and R. Worden April 26, 2006

220

MODOT Environmental Specialist Alan Leary went down a steep grade into the so-called Stowell Cave, the air thick with the smell of damp clay and rock. While exploring the cave, he made an exciting discovery—a man-created symbol had been painted or drawn on the wall. "There's a circle, and then a line, and then an arrow," he said, noting the symbol did not appear to be spray-painted. Leary believed it was a directional symbol left for cavers in the past. "It points back to the end of the passage. It would seem as though that passage used to go further, because it would have made no sense to point an arrow twenty feet from the end." Clearly, someone had been in the passage and drawn an arrow to find their way back out to the surface. "There used to be an opening to this cave somewhere around here. At one time it could have been linked with a large cave system," Leary theorized to reporters.

He described the cave passage as being about fifty feet long and located twenty feet below the surface. Inside, he found some calcite speleothems and a few crickets and beetles. He noted the sediment and clay floor was damp, indicating the cave takes on water regularly, possibly even filling the passage. "It's a tall cave," Leary reported, "tall enough you can walk, but we did have to crawl over some mud."

Small spurs extended from the main passage, but these were heavily silted from water moving through the passages over eons.

The cave entrance was temporarily closed until further evaluation could be made. The following week, MODOT had a skilled team of cavers further explore the new passages.

The decision was made to bring expert cavers to the scene to both document its characteristics and ensure there were no signs of the missing boys. "Obviously there's a lot of passion about what the area means, and it's always something we've kept in the back of our minds as we've worked around here," said Dave Sylvester, a MODOT engineer.

Craig Dowell's half brother, Bill Dean, had come to the scene still holding out hope for some good news. "It's been forty years and they just disappeared off the face of the earth. There's a few of us that want some answers," he told a *Quincy Herald-Whig* reporter.

Joining Leary in this second foray were: Jim Kaufmann, a cave ecologist with the Missouri Department of Conservation; Jeffrey Crews, president of the Missouri Speleological Society; and Rita Worden, a cave expert from the University of Missouri-Columbia. The three experienced cavers mapped the new discovery to add to the state's massive cave file database. They were surprised to find three drawn arrows on the cave walls, describing them as typical symbols used by cavers decades ago. Leary commented they may have been drawn during the 1967 search. "It is a typical directional marking for underground exploration."

In all, three entrances were found. Two led to the same cave and a third was a geologic pocket that did not extend very far. These three openings were soon filled, and the new Stowell School was built with Fulton Avenue redirected around it. Progress marched on, but, once again, no sign of the boys had been found, and Hannibal area residents suffered another wave of disappointment.

Chapter 12

Teen Risk

Wesley Tischer, who was a ninth grader in 1967, knew all three missing boys. Like so many other Hannibal youngsters, Wes had the cultural genetics of Tom Sawyer, exploring the town's hills and caves. But the unsuccessful search for Joel, Billy, and Craig taught Hannibal's children a lesson.

"Growing up in the fifties and sixties on the Southside, we all explored," Tischer said. "When the boys went missing it told us we were not invincible. You know, when you're in middle school you think you're invincible. Well, that incident really gave us something to think about." Tischer said his parents had issued a stern edict. "Our folks told us, 'No more caves, period.' I honored that and never again had any desire to go into a cave unless it was a guided tour of a show cave."

Half a century later, Tischer's a semi-retired pastor who still reflects back on the cave search and the grief left in its wake. "As a pastor you understand grief. What happened in Hannibal was worse than death, three kids just never coming home again and their families having no closure. I just can't imagine going through a calamity like that with no closure. It's just a tragic mystery."

"The missing boys reminds me of the old saying," Tischer reflected, "one boy is a boy, two is half a boy and three is no boy at all. That's the truth, too." In other words, it is easy to get one boy to focus on a task, but when there are two, there is distraction, and with three, the distraction or propensity for danger or chaos increases dramatically. Three boys, given the right circumstances, can be a fatal mix.

What is it about boys and risk? On many occasions, in 1873, 1961, and finally in 1967, kids went missing in Hannibal caves. And, not to single out Missouri, similar events have happened worldwide over the decades. Thankfully, most amateur spelunkers in trouble are rescued or eventually find their own way out into the sunlight.

But for these Hannibal boys, modern-day Tom Sawyers, the caves were so enticing their better judgement was overridden by the promise of adventure. It seemed they had completely lost or disregarded any sense of risk. There was a boldness, a fearlessness that manifested to drive their decision-making. Today, neuroscientists know much more about the teenage brain than they did in the 1960s. Many psychologists will tell you that three boys will do what two might never consider.

We all understand that adolescence is an awkward time. Teens are at an age of self-discovery, developing independence and seeking peer acceptance while withdrawing from reliance on their parents. Risk-taking seems to come with the territory as brain development continues until the mid-twenties with different portions of the brain maturing at different rates.

Teens find themselves in an anxiety-prone period with their brains seemingly out of sync. Here's why: The amygdala, the brain's fear and response center, develops ahead of the prefrontal cortex, the portion of the brain that drives reasoning and self-control. As a result, teenagers are less able to control their emotions and responses and remain more prone to take risks, especially in situations where peer pressure is prominent. The developing teenage brain creates a risk-taking vulnerability that peaks about the time the child experiences puberty, the behavioral balance tipping in favor of high emotion and risky behavior. The teen finds it hard to resist as the key portions of the brain involved with impulse control and risky behavior won't be fully developed until they're nearly twenty-five.

That's why the death rate for teens fifteen to nineteen is nearly twice the rate for toddlers and preschoolers. Teenagers must endure this statistical "accident hump," when they're prone to speeding, experimenting with drugs and alcohol, and succumbing to other reckless behaviors.

Cognitive scientists have found that kids are more likely to take risks when they are together. A teenage driver with other teens in the vehicle is four times as likely to crash as a teenager who drives alone. Crime rates begin to rise steeply around age thirteen and peak at age eighteen. This statistical age-crime curve reflects the impulsiveness of teenagers unwilling and, to an extent, unable to moderate and temper their reckless behavior.

The teenage brain is heavily influenced by Dopamine, the neurotransmitter involved in reward behavior, and brain levels of this chemical peak during adolescence when they're growing more independent and need motivation to take new chances and try new things. It's a precarious balance for teens to maintain.

Thankfully, by the time they are in their early twenties, self-control will take precedence over emotional arousal and risky behavior.

One study conducted by psychology Professor Laurence Steinberg at Temple University found that teens take more risks when kids their age are with them. Being watched stimulates the brain's reward center and this affect is highest when teens know there's a high probability that something bad might happen, according to Steinberg.

In other words, teens underestimate risk and overestimate reward. MRI brain scans, he said, show a highly stimulated, dopamine-fueled brain when a teen believes someone else is watching what they're doing.

Teen Girls

How do teenage girls fare in the risk arena? In conducting research for this book, I heard not one instance of a girl exploring the exposed maze caves. Cognitive scientists now know why.

Studies show that teenage boys are more prone to making riskier decisions than girls in the same age group. Given an overall higher activity level, boys often behave more impulsively than girls. There are environmental factors to consider, too. One study in the Journal of Pediatric Psychology (Vol. 23, No. 1, 1, 1998) states: "Parents are less likely to restrain the exploratory behavior of boys than girls. Similarly, boys are allowed to roam further from home... which would result in boys receiving less direct supervision than girls," wrote University of Guelph researchers Barbara Morrongiello, PhD, and Heather Rennie, MSc.

While boys are often unable to avoid a threat, even when told not to do so, girls are better able to assess all available information about a threat and make a decision based on wariness. The *wary effect* is much stronger for teen girls than boys. Girls simply sense perceived risks better and more quickly assess their confidence level in being able to complete risky activities. Boys show more of an optimism bias, being less inclined to factor in peer concerns about executing a risky activity. "...the best predictor of girls' intentions to take risk was their perceived vulnerability for injury... whereas for boys it was perceived severity of injury (i.e., beliefs about how hurt they might get)."

The teenage years represent a busy time for brain development, and two of the three lost boys were, cognitively speaking, at ground zero.

Maybe that's why Craig, Joel, and Billy explored the roadcut caves, despite abundant warning from parents and the Highway 79 construction workers. Each boy, perhaps, wanted to appear brave and heroic—fearless—in the eyes of the other two.

National Guard Commander Bill Tucker who led the Hannibal ground search believes two boys would not have acted the same as three. "Joel and Billy were followers, in my view. If it had been just the two of them they may not have gone into the caves. The Dowell kid was older and perhaps he assumed leadership. That's my take," said the military leader.

The lost boys fell prey to adolescent development, rejecting obviously sound warnings from caring, reasoning adults and boldly going forward into a dangerous destiny.

Chapter 13

A Vexing Mystery

After the historic, nearly month-long Hannibal search of an estimated 270 caves and many miles of countryside, not a shred of solid evidence was ever found about the boys' whereabouts.

News coverage nationally, and as far away as Australia and Vietnam, failed to flush out any additional clues. Now missing half a century, it is unknown what happened to Joel Hoag, thirteen, his brother Billy, eleven, and their friend, fourteen-year-old Edwin Craig Dowell. The case remains open, a remarkable unsolved mystery.

Due to the high-profile search and worldwide news coverage, the three boys made more friends than they ever could have fathomed. If only Joel, Billy and Craig could have met them all. Even now friends ask, "Do you still think about May of '67?" "Yes, all the time, when I drive the area or visit Hannibal, or read about a missing child," I answer.

Missouri caver and speleohistorian Dwight Weaver believes the Hannibal search is unique in modern history. "The Hannibal search is probably the most vexing Missouri cave mystery of our times." He added, "If the missing boys had been in any cave passage even remotely accessible to a human being, I feel confident that the cavers would have found them. Missouri cavers are among the most persistent, innovative and skilled cavers in America."

In his after-action report about the Hannibal cave search, Speleological Society of America President William Karras wrote, "What then, did happen to the boys? My heart cries because we failed to find the boys. It would be better to believe they just went away. I'm at as much a loss why God put this mystery before us as anyone."

After the search, the Highway 79 roadcut system was formally named Lost Boys Cave by the Missouri Speleological Survey. The memorialized cave's many openings were closed, and at dinner tables throughout the city Hannibal's children were told by their parents to forget the latticed-cave network below.

Karras' cave rescue organization, the Speleological Society of America, disbanded in 1969 three years after it had been established. Financial issues and political infighting within the cave community had taken a toll after Karras' record of controversial cave search and rescue incidents. But Garland Black, a founding SSA member, sees it differently. "Despite what was said, we all believed in one national caving organization. The SSA ended when the National Speleological Society decided to create a national cave search and rescue program. At that point we were all in agreement, so we closed the SSA."

Black said the Hannibal operation took Karras and his men to their absolute limits. "The SSA team members were all exhausted physically and mentally, very sad they could not find anything. Karras lost a lot of weight, he lost four inches off his waist. Bill came back home, physically and mentally exhausted. He said it had been exceptionally hard work. He told me, 'God have mercy on their souls. We have to let God handle it, we've done all we could.' He did everything possible to find them," Black added.

Black said Karras told him he thought someone had taken the boys and killed them, despite a lack of evidence at the time to support such a theory.

After Hannibal, Karras changed his focus from the subterranean world to other endeavors. Always an adventurer, Karras sold snowmobiles in the 1970s and reportedly became the first person to drive a Skidoo brand sled across the United States.

Later, he embraced a long-time aviation interest and pursued hot air ballooning in the Pacific Northwest where he started a business—Hot Air Productions—crafting gondolas and balloons. He even achieved the record books for his greatest ballooning achievement. On May 31, 1981, Karras and his co-pilot Scott Gardiner accomplished the first crossing of the Cascade Mountains by hot air balloon. Taking advantage of rare easterly winds, the two men launched from Issaquah, east of Seattle at 12:50 p.m. Four previous attempts at the ninety-mile crossing by other balloonists had been unsuccessful.

The men took their massive balloon, the Shenandoah, eighty feet high and sixty-five feet in diameter, up to thirteen thousand feet where they found their sweet spot, as forty-mile-per-hour winds aligned with their flight path. Karras, then fifty-seven, had accrued more than two thousand hours of experience piloting balloons in the previous decade. As captain of the flight, he expressed exuberant confidence they would be successful. About five p.m., the Shenandoah floated over 12,307-foot Mount Adams and began its descent, landing seven miles north of the Yakima, Washington airport. The record-setting adventure had taken four hours.

A Washington state hot air balloonist and tour manager for musical acts like Bonnie Raitt and Jackson Browne, a man who goes by the single name of Kong, had first met Karras as a fourteen-year-old boy with a budding interest in hot air ballooning. Kong developed a warm friendship with Karras and his wife Janelle. "Bill was a pretty amazing individual. He was a genuine adventurer and a dreamer who made his dreams come true," Kong said. "He was an inspiring mentor and always had young people around, very likeable, and a legend in Northwest hot air ballooning circles."

Karras kept his eyes to the sky, later becoming interested in ultra-light aircraft, but trouble found him. On May 29, 1983, Karras was piloting an Eipper Quicksilver MX ultra-light aircraft near a Memorial Day crowd at a park in Sumner, Washington. Witnesses, according to the *National Transportation Safety Board Aviation Accident Summary*, said Karras' aircraft had performed wing-over maneuvers over the lake and was making a second pass when the engine suddenly stopped.

In a momentary panic, Karras quickly reached over his head to restart the engine. The ultra-light aircraft had two fuel tanks, and he noticed the main tank was empty. Karras struggled to open the petcock knob on the other tank to restore fuel flow, but while distracted for these chaotic few seconds the aircraft struck a tree. Karras sustained serious eye and head injuries.

Later, battling bladder cancer, vision troubles and neurological issues, William Karras spent his final years living with his wife in nursing homes in Kansas, where Janelle had grown up.

I telephoned Karras a few years before his death. The weak, high pitched voice that answered the phone revealed a frail man now facing new struggles as his wife, Janelle, battled multiple sclerosis. He didn't talk long, but acknowledged the frustration everyone still feels about the outcome of the Hannibal operation: "It's a real mystery where those boys are. We did our very best to find them. I still think about it."

William Gus Karras died on his eightieth birthday, February 22, 2004, at the Halstead Health & Rehab, a skilled care center in Halstead, Kansas. "Near the end, he slept a lot and finally just dwindled away," said Kent Haury, Janelle's brother.

Karras, who had spent so much of his life in a dark underworld of caverns, had stepped into eternal light and hopefully attained all the answers to the mystery that had dogged him for decades.

Tex Yokum, who served as the director for the SSA's Great Plains Region, wrote after the search: "Unless you were an active participant in this massive search, it will be impossible for you to understand the complexities of a project of this size. Never in the history of caving have cavers engaged in a search as mysterious as this. As far as I know, in every other rescue, operations could be concentrated at one point, since it was known precisely where to look, but not so in this case." Yokum reported the search had thoroughly targeted a seven-mile radius of Hannibal's city limits, the scope of which had never before been encountered by a cave rescue unit.

"My only regret," Yokum wrote, "is that we came away empty-handed. It is extremely distressing when you realize that with all the talent, energy, time, equipment and money expended in this search, we failed to find one single shred of physical evidence concerning the boys." The experienced Missouri caver, now deceased, called the historic search a "tremendous test of our ingenuity, stamina, dedication and ability to cooperate."

The former Deputy State Geologist, Jerry Vineyard, who died in March 2017 before publication of this book, was involved in cave identification, exploration, and conservation his entire professional life. His belief? "After a while, it became pretty apparent to me that the boys had not run away, and they were not in any other known open caves because we had checked. I think they were under the road and they're still there, if we only knew *where*."

Vineyard speculated that the boys could have been in a passage on the western fringe of the roadcut when a collapse sealed them away preventing their escape. "I think whatever happened, happened suddenly with the three boys grouped together." This is the very scenario teacher Louise Kohler's psychic mother had sensed the evening of May 12. "That roadcut had been drilled and shot (dynamited) and basically was an accident waiting to happen," Vineyard recalled. "They had all this shot rock and openings into it, so I'm convinced the boys went into one of the openings and, while they were in there, the roof fell in on them, and we were just never able to find that spot."

That is the viewpoint from Missouri's contemporary "Father of Caving." Vineyard visited Hannibal many years after the search and was struck by how ordinary the area appeared. "The highway department had concreted up the entrances that were on the east side of Highway 79. The area appeared strangely benign compared to having looked very dangerous in 1967 with everything open and raw. Now, vegetation has grown up and weathering has softened the roadcut features," Vineyard said.

The Hondo team from St. Louis remained in Hannibal for ten days after Karras departed, continuing the search, and some members would periodically return in the following months. Christensen, who at the time of the Hannibal search worked for McDonnell-Douglas, the builder of the F-4 Phantom fighter aircrafts, left the aerospace giant in 1972 to become a commercial printer. He continued his caving activities for many years after Hannibal.

Susan DeVier, the petite caver who helped explore some of the smaller passages in Murphy's Cave, eventually remarried and had children. Now Susan Baker, she and her husband enjoy the quiet serenity of their 120 rural acres in northern Moniteau County. While Susan eventually left caving, caving has not left her. Their property includes Bruce Cave, a popular subterranean destination for Boy Scout troops and science clubs from area schools. "It's an easy cave," Susan explained, "...pretty much a straight shot with a sinkhole and crawl-way to keep it interesting."

Half a century later, Susan's thoughts occasionally turn to Hannibal, her first and last cave search operation. "After I returned home, the search affected me for quite a while. It was very intense and there was just no closure. It must have been ungodly for the families to see everyone pack up and just leave town." Even now, the frustration is evident in her voice. "Once in a great while I'll think about it. I gave it my all and did the best I could... we all did. There was just nothing more to be done."

Susan says her take-away from the whole experience is a gut-wrenching thought that has never left her: "The worst thing in the world is to not know what happened to a loved one, to know only that they vanished, never to be seen again. That's hard for the families, and it's hard for all of us."

Carbondale caver Joe Walsh, who's been in hundreds of caves, still finds the Hannibal case baffling. "The opinion of many of the cavers is that the boys were not in the caves. Many believed the boys were either abducted or ran off. But we don't really *know*."

Bob Cowder, the caver and Missouri National Guard platoon leader who helped with the ground search, quickly grew frustrated by the lack of success during the search and in the years that followed. "Nobody really knows what happened, but everyone has a theory," he lamented. "There was just no trace whatsoever of those three young boys. It was just remarkable. That just doesn't happen. The interest was feverish for a while and just died down because there was nothing to sustain it." Cowder suspects the boys may have met foul play. In an eighteen-month period, he said, two Quincy women and two individuals from Monroe City had disappeared. "One of the women was found dead in the river bottoms near Quincy. There just seemed to be a lot of disappearances in the area during that time." It was more fodder, but no concrete leads, to fuel the mystery surrounding Hannibal's lost boys.

Woody St. Clair, a member of the Mark Twain Emergency Squad in 1967, believes the boys were lost in Murphy's Cave. "I was a coroner for twenty years and an undertaker for ten years. What I smelled at Murphy's Cave several days into the search was a *human* odor. Once you smell it you don't forget it. That's my theory, and a lot of others agree. I think something caved in on them and they died quickly. It's a shame we never found them." Woody had befriended brothers Fred and Tim Hoag during the search and remained friends for decades until their deaths. "Over time, they talked less and less about what happened in 1967. It was just too painful."

John Lyng, the newspaper intern who would be elected Hannibal mayor years later, believes the search was too focused on Murphy's Cave initially. "Everyone was primarily looking there when they should have checked the roadcut sooner and more intensely."

Ruth Martin-Ellison, whose father was pastor at Southside Christian Church for years, still lives in Hannibal with her husband. She takes an eternal perspective. "I've always said when I get to Heaven, one of the first things I'm going to ask is what happened to the boys. It has haunted us for years."

Gary Rush, a lifelong Hannibal resident and a friend of mine since age four, finds his thoughts often turning to the lost boys' search. "I would have likely been with them going into the caves May 10, but I had a guitar lesson that evening. Every time I read something about the disappearances over these many years, it touches emotions. It's haunted me I guess, that it could have been me, too."

Rush believes the boys went into a roadbed opening and were unknowingly buried and trapped by the heavy equipment rumbling down the dusty highway construction site filling in cave openings to stabilize the roadbed. "People came from all over the country to this little town to help us, it was extraordinary. They say time heals all things, but some things you never really ever get over. When we get to Heaven, perhaps we'll know the whole story," Rush said.

Payson, Illinois caver David Mahon noted that the east side of Murphy's Cave was very dangerous in his opinion. "Those first passages that ran parallel with the hillside surface were unstable." That was due to surface erosion and rainfall. "I think they were trapped in Murphy's Cave," Mahon said. "They could have gotten into a small passage, too small for adults to search, and there was a collapse. Remember, a good portion of Murphy's Cave remained unmapped and unsearched due to many small, unreachable passages."

Jim Arrigo, the Wentzville machinist and caver, says he'll never forgot how so many people selflessly committed to a shared purpose. "It was so amazing how people came together, especially the people in Hannibal. It was something to witness. People gave whatever they had, whether it was money or meals or pure determined grit to get in there and look for the boys. It was inspiring."

On the drive home, Jim fought fatigue from the exhausting three days he'd spent searching. "It was sad having to go back home to my wife and tell her we didn't do any good. Where were the boys? There was just no resolve to the question, really. We tried the best we knew how, but there was just no sign of them."

"We had high hopes, when we first got there, that we'd find them. But once we saw the roadcut, doubt started entering our minds because you could see the danger that was involved. If the boys were below the roadcut any hopes were pretty well dashed. They found their resting place, I'm sure. It was a sad, sad deal," Arrigo said.

Retired Missouri National Guard Commander Colonel Bill Tucker believes the missing boys made Hannibal as famous as Mark Twain had done many decades earlier. "With that memorial stone up on Lover's Leap, people who come to Hannibal go look at it and think about this terrible event."

The Hannibal event birthed an historic story of tragedy and heroism. Craig Dowell's surviving family members would not publicly speak about the tragedy, but clearly the pain and grief remain very real. They, too, have our prayers.

The Hoag family experienced more pain than most families could ever be expected to bear. After Billy and Joel went missing, another son, Mikey (Michael Terry Hoag, Jr.) was killed in a February 1968 car accident in Columbia, South Carolina. He was enroute to his annual physical health checkup when another vehicle crossed the center line and struck Mikey's car head-on. He was pronounced dead at the scene. The driver and passenger in the other car were unhurt, but reportedly inebriated. Moonshine was found in their car. Mikey, who's greatest desire had been to work in law enforcement, briefly achieved that dream. He was buried at twenty-five, three months shy of his twenty-sixth birthday, with the badge he'd so proudly worn.

In October 1975, another Hoag son, Robin, who adored Joel and Billy and was their "little buddy," died in a tragic shooting at age sixteen. "The disappearance of Joey and Billy had taken a toll on him that no one fully realized," said sister Lynnie Hoag-Pedigo.

Helen and Michael Hoag's family had lost three sons and brothers in nine months, then a fourth seven years later. Tragedy heaped upon tragedy. We wish them peace.

For years after the Hannibal tragedy, according to a daughter, Helen Hoag would sit in her living room at night staring at the front door, hoping Billy and Joel would come bouncing in, enthusiastic and full of life. Her expectant behavior was justified. During the Great Depression, Helen's Uncle George vanished and remained missing for seventeen years. "He had apparently stolen a loaf of bread and scared of getting into trouble ran off," explained Lynnie Hoag-Pedigo. George was finally found by Prudential Insurance Company investigators while processing an insurance claim related to his suspected death. "He returned home after being gone all that time and resumed his life with Aunt Grace. So Mom had seen this play out before. She still had hope."

In November 1989, Helen and the kids gathered around Mike Hoag as he lay on his deathbed. "When he passed," Lynnie explained, "I told Mom, Dad knows now." Helen nodded quiet agreement. Helen died in June 1995 after a life of hardship and pain, yet one tempered by much love. "During the Great Depression, Mom was just five when her own mother had miscarried at home and, fearful of hospitals, died of infection," Lynnie said. "It was hard for her growing up, eating table scraps during tight times, and going barefoot in the summer to save wear and tear on her one pair of shoes. She was a very good mother of eleven children for not having had a mother to teach her."

Helen Hoag had once told Lynnie, "God loaned you kids to me and I don't know for how long."

Lynnie has come to accept the terms of the family's sad fate. "We're apparently not to know what happened to them. We have to trust in God. I've found relief in that over these years and can live in peace with it. My brothers are in God's hands."

She quickly grows emotional reflecting on the heroic efforts by hundreds of people to locate the boys. "People took off work and came to search everywhere. They were just so wonderful. You can't believe their compassion and how they reached out to help. It was so heroic."

And to this day, Lynnie is steadfast and remains ever hopeful about the boys' fate. "Missing, not deceased," she tells herself.

"You really don't ever get over it," said another Hoag sister to a FOX News reporter in 2017. I really have a hard time dealing with it. Time just goes on and on, and you pray, you try to get an answer. There isn't a day that goes by that there isn't something that makes me think about them. I've got to have closure, but we haven't found a thing."

The psychological trauma surrounding the Hannibal event was etched into the psyche, leaving in its wake indelible traumatic memories that continue to intrude, even after half a century.

The boys had lost their futures and earthly hopes, their potential to step into their fathers' shoes gone. We grieve precious sons, brothers and friends. The emotional wounds never fully healed, only scabbed over. The heartache endures.

It has been a bittersweet journey. In the past fifty years, those of us blessed with longevity have gone on to build careers, marry and raise our own children. And we've carried the memories of the lost boys with us. We knew them only a little while, but their flames burned brightly. We were touched by their curiosity, exuberance and joy while they were among us—childhood friendships we'll never forget.

Mark Twain wrote in his autobiography, "The human family cannot be described by any one phrase; each individual has to be described by himself. One is brave, another is a coward; one is gentle and kindly, another is ferocious; one is proud and vain, another is modest and humble."

Had Mark Twain been blessed to know the more than two hundred cavers and other search volunteers in Hannibal, he would surely have ordained them brave, dedicated and heroic men and women. They will never be forgotten as history continues to honor the lost boys—Joel, Billy and Craig—and all of the selfless participants who were swept up in the historic high drama to find them in America's Hometown.

State Highway 79 roadcut area after completion. Photo by John Wingate

Postscript

Two More Theories

Throughout the decades, many Hannibalians have wondered whether the boys were victims of abduction and murder. As the Hoag family had no car, the boys were known to accept rides from total strangers to get across town or down to Mark Twain Cave, behavior the Hoag parents had warned the boys about many times.

While police had no evidence of foul play, many people wondered whether the boys could have been victims of monster serial killer John Wayne Gacy.

Beginning in 1972, Gacy assaulted, tortured and murdered thirty-three—perhaps more—teenage boys and young men. His known victims were murdered in his suburban Chicago home after he had lured them there by deception or force. Twenty-six of the victims were buried in the crawl space under his house. Three others were buried elsewhere on the property. Four were dumped in the Des Plaines River.

Gacy was caught, convicted and served prison time until his death by lethal injection at Illinois' Stateville Correctional Center on May 10, 1994, coincidentally the same month and day the lost boys had gone missing twenty-seven years earlier.

In the years since, Cook County Sheriff's Department detectives have worked tirelessly to identify Gacy's victims. As of the publication of this book, only six victims remain unidentified.

Over the past decades, detectives have taken DNA samples from the surviving relatives of young male missing persons and entered the results into the National Crime Information Center's (NCIC) Combined DNA Index (CODIS), the federal database operated by the FBI and linked with law enforcement agencies nationwide. In more than two dozen cases, Chicago authorities have matched samples with DNA from Gacy's victims, enabling law enforcement authorities to finally close many missing person cases and bring closure for the families.

After Gacy was arrested, the Hoag family—and many others— wondered if Gacy had been in Hannibal on May 10, 1967. It was a long shot, but stranger things have happened. Who would have thought three missing boys would never be found.

St. Louis area policeman Daniel Jack Hoag, the brother of Mike Hoag, father of Joel and Billy, needed to know the answers to questions that persisted in his mind. Had Gacy been in the Hannibal area in May 1967? Had the lost boys been abducted and murdered by him, their final resting place located somewhere in the Chicago area? Is it possible Hannibal's lost boys had been prey for one of the most notoriously evil serial killers of the twentieth century?

Hannibal native Steve Sederwall, a lifelong law enforcement officer, who now resides in Lincoln County, New Mexico where he investigates cold criminal cases, discovered some intriguing information from Cook County detectives still working to close the books on Gacy's murder victims' identities.

"Gacy kept detailed records of his travels. Police say his travels around 1967 may have taken him to the Ladonia, Missouri area," Sederwall said. Ladonia is forty-one miles from Hannibal. At the time, Gacy was living in Waterloo, a four-hour drive from Hannibal.

In 1966, Gacy reportedly had relocated to Waterloo to manage three Kentucky Fried Chicken restaurants owned by his father-in-law. It was a heady time. Gacy had landed a lucrative job, joined the local Jaycees, and helped with local fundraising projects. In

1967, he was named "Outstanding Vice President" of the Waterloo Jaycees. Gacy's wife gave birth to a son in early 1966 and a daughter in March 1967. Gacy was building a family, hoping it would be a happier one than his own.

In 1966, Gacy's parents visited Waterloo. During the visit, his father reportedly apologized for the physical and mental abuse he had inflicted upon John Wayne throughout childhood. When Gacy was younger, his father saw something in his personality that was concerning. Feeling a good spanking was therapeutic, the father administered the rod regularly. Now, visiting his son in Waterloo, he could only say, "Son, I was wrong about you."

While the abuse had ended long ago, the seeds of trauma were growing in a dark corner of Gacy's mind. While in Waterloo, Gacy's true nature began to reveal itself. He cheated on his wife with prostitutes and operated a club in his basement for teenage employees of his restaurants. Some were offered alcohol before Gacy made sexual advances, and when rebuffed, Gacy would laugh off the behavior as being a joke. In March 1968, the teenage son of a Jaycee member told his father Gacy had assaulted him the previous summer. Gacy was indicted on a sodomy charge on May 10, 1968, oddly, *exactly* one year after the boys went missing in Hannibal. A court-ordered psychiatric evaluation concluded Gacy had Antisocial Personality Disorder, and given his psychopathic tendencies was unlikely to benefit from therapy or treatment. The psychiatrist's conclusion? Police had not heard the last of John Wayne Gacy as his behaviors would likely continue to conflict with the norms of a civilized society. Gacy was convicted of the sodomy charge and sentenced to ten years at the Anamosa State Penitentiary near Cedar Rapids, Iowa. His wife filed for divorce and Gacy never saw her and their two children again.

In prison, Gacy was a model prisoner; he helped operate the prison Jaycee chapter and took classes to finally earn his high school diploma. When his abusive father died on Christmas day 1969, Gacy reportedly collapsed and sobbed uncontrollably. His request for a temporary release to attend his father's funeral was denied.

In June 1970, Gacy won parole and moved to Chicago to live with his mother. He joined the Democratic Party and got involved in civic activities, being named director of the annual Polish Constitution Day Parade. It was through his work with the parade that he met and was photographed with First Lady Rosalynn Carter, a photo she surely wishes could be erased from history. Once reestablished in Chicago, Gacy's serial killing spree got underway as the dark corner of his mind emerged, driving his evil and deadly rages.

Sederwall wondered if Gacy could have been the mystery man who lingered at the roadcut watching the Highway 79 road construction activities. As it turns out, Sederwall and Daniel Jack Hoag were cut from the same cloth, sharing a curious persistence for truth. In August 2017, we learned that in the early 1980s, officer Hoag had gathered the dental records for the Hoag and Dowell boys and submitted them to Cook County investigators. "They reviewed and compared the dental records with those of Gacy's known victims and found there was no match," said Lynnie Hoag-Pedigo.

But is this the end of the story? Could Gacy have killed the boys and buried them elsewhere in graves that have not yet been discovered?

Sederwall traveled to Missouri in August 2017 where he met with a Hannibal Police representative. "My goal is simple," Sederwall said. "Let's collect DNA samples from the surviving Hoag and Dowell siblings and enter the data into the NCIC-CODIS system. This way, when any unidentified remains anywhere are discovered in the future, police might get a hit that would possibly identify any remains as those of the lost boys."

Coincidentally, the NCIC federal database first became operational as a crime-solving tool in May 1967. Soon, detailed family genetic information common to the lost boys will hopefully be included in this massive DNA database in the hopes that, had they been crime victims, their remains might one day be identified and put to eternal rest, bringing closure to these beleaguered families.

But, for now, the Gacy theory is just that—one more theory in the sad saga of Hannibal's lost boys.

***

The nearby viaduct, constructed in 1967, that delivers traffic over Bear Creek near Murphy's Cave has come under suspicion in recent years. Dan Bledsoe is now a retired radio host who lives in Las Vegas, Nevada. For decades, he met and interviewed many top country music stars. In May 1967, young Dan and his family lived at 704 Birch street, near Murphy's Cave and the viaduct. His late father, Leo, was a Hannibal postal service employee and an amateur photographer. "He loved photography," Bledsoe said in his deep, resonant voice. "We still have several thousand slides of his. He really enjoyed taking photos around town."

During the road construction project, Mr. Bledsoe took his 35mm Canon film camera and documented both the road construction activity, which took several feet of the family's front yard, and the cave search efforts. Several of the slides he took of the Murphy's Cave search are used in this book; all of the images are in pristine condition and appear to have been taken only yesterday.

Dan Bledsoe's mother and siblings at the Birch Street viaduct, May 1967.

The day before the lost boys went missing, Leo Bledsoe had seen the trio by the viaduct, precariously standing on narrow boards that spanned a gap between the dusty Birch street roadbed and the viaduct's deck. The boards spanned a six-foot gap over tall forms that were in place, ready for concrete to be poured. "My feeling has always been that maybe the boards weren't all that firm. If all three of the boys walked across the boards at once and they broke, they would fall into the deep concrete forms," Dan Bledsoe theorized. Such a fall, perhaps thirty feet or more, would likely be fatal or cause serious injury. Deep in the inky darkness of the forms, would cries for help from injured boys be heard, if they were even able to scream? Would the forms be visually checked internally before concrete was poured?

Leo Bledsoe happened to take a photo of three boys standing on the boards spanning the Birch-viaduct gap on May 9 or 10. "Dad usually had Tuesday or Wednesday as a day off, and that's when he would photograph the activity," Bledsoe said. After the boys went missing, Dan's father remembered the photo and retrieved it to show Dan and the rest of the family. The whereabouts of this slide is currently unknown. "He shot thousands of color slides, and each time I go to Kansas City to visit family, I sit and review more of them," Bledsoe said. "I'll keep looking. I want to find that image. It's proof the boys had been playing around the viaduct."

Again, one more theory.

Resources

Karras, William G., *The Hannibal Story, Speleological Society of America* after-action report, SSA Speleologist, December 1967

Hannibal Courier Post newspaper clippings, May 1967

Quincy Herald-Whig newspaper clippings, May 1967

45 Years Missing, Hannibal Courier Post reporter interview with Debbie Hoag, https://www.youtube.com/watch?v=sZpyzDTo_uQ, May 28, 2012

Weaver, H. Dwight. Mark Twain Cave: The Most Celebrated Cave in American Literature, The Donning Company Publishers, 2017

Lohraff, Kevin. *Hiking Missouri*, Human Kinetics, 2009

St. Louis Post-Dispatch news clippings, May 1967

St. Louis Globe-Democrat news clippings, May 1967

Kansas City Star newspaper, news clippings, May-June 1967

Pittsburg Post-Gazette, May 12, 1967

Collins, Homer, Lehrberger, John L., *The Life and Death of Floyd Collins*, Cave Books, 2001

Andrews, Gregg, City of Dust: A Cement Company Town in the Land of Tom Sawyer, University of Missouri Press, 1996

Tabor, James, Blind Descent: The Quest to Discover the Deepest Place on Earth, Random House, 2010

National Speleological Society, Wikipedia background

Bretz, J. Harlen, Caves of Missouri, State of Missouri Department of Business and Administration Division of Geological Survey and Water Resources, 1956

Schaper, Jo, *10,000 Years of Caving in Missouri*, Webster's Home Cave http://members.socket.net/~joschaper/webster.html

Hoppin, Ruth, Cave Animals from Southwestern Missouri, Bulletin of Comparative Zoology Vol. 16-17, Museum of Comparative Zoology, 1889

Fowke, Gerald, *Cave Explorations in the Ozark Region of Central Missouri*, Smithsonian Institution Bureau of American Ethnology Bulletin 76, Government Printing Office, 1922

Mueller, Doris Land, *Daring to be Different: Missouri's Remarkable Owen Sisters*, University of Missouri Press, 2010

Owen, Luella, Cave Regions of the Ozarks and Black Hills, 1898, Johnson Reprint Corporation, 1970

Hovey, Dr. H.C., *Celebrated American Caverns*, Robert Clarke & Company, 1882

Vineyard, Jerry, *J. Harlen Bretz in Missouri*, Missouri Speleology Vol. 19 3-4, Missouri Speleological Survey, Inc., 1979

Weaver, H. Dwight, *Missouri Caves in History and Legend*, University of Missouri Press, Columbia, Missouri, 2008

Keefe, Amanda, *Lost in a Perry County cave*, Perryville Republic-Monitor, December 12, 2013

Weaver, H. Dwight, Mark Twain Cave : The Most Celebrated Cave In American Literature, The Donning Company Publishers, 2017

Weaver, H. Dwight, Adventures at Mark Twain Cave: The Discovery, History and Development of the Cave, Discovery Enterprises, 1972

Twain, Mark, *The Adventures of Tom Sawyer*, American Publishing Company, Hartford, Connecticut, 1876

Searching a cave for three Tom Sawyers, LIFE magazine, May 26, 1967

Berry, James R., *How They Rescued Me 200 Feet Underground*, Popular Science, October 1965

Heartbreak and Gallantry in Hannibal's Hills, editorial in the Kansas City Star, May 23, 1967

Ulrich, Michael, *Tight Squeeze*, Guidepost magazine, May 1995

Ohio Cave Sealed After Boy's Rescue, The Sandusky Register, October 7, 1965

Boy Trapped in Medina Cave Rescued After 24 Hour Ordeal, Associated Press, October 7, 1965

Four Men Trapped In Cave, Arkansas Gazette, April 5, 1965

Rising Waters Trap Four in Ozark Mountain Cave, Chicago Tribune, April 5, 1965

Downey, Tim, The Schroeder's Pants Cave Tragedy: What Really Happened & What Happened After, NSS News, August 2007

Chemist's remains recovered from cave, The Buffalo News/Associated Press, June 25, 2006

Jackson, Gordon, *Finally, closure on failed rescue*, The Florida Times-Union, July 3, 2006

Speece, Jack H., *Schroeder's Cave*, Presentation at National Speleological Society convention in Albuquerque, New Mexico, June 2017

Anderson, Shawn, *Out of the dark, into the light*, Utica Observer-Dispatch, June 30, 2006

Reppert, Ralph, *Experts in the Dangerous Art of Cave Rescues*, Baltimore Sun, January 9, 1966

Origin and Early History of the S.S.A, Central Indiana Grotto newsletter, March 1967

Finch, Wayne, *Fiasco in Hannibal*, Middle Mississippi Valley Grotto newsletter, June 1967

American Caving Accidents, National Speleological Society, 1967

Caving in America: The story of the National Speleological Society 1941-1991, National Speleological Society, 1991

Speece, Jack H., *William Karras and the Speleological Society of America*, presentation at the 2008 NSS convention in Lake City, Florida, 2008

Webster, Detective Charles, *official police report*, Hannibal Police Department, November 15, 1995

Hunold, Lt. Joe, *official police report*, Hannibal Police Department, November 16, 1995

Clark, Margie, *Police close investigation into boys' disappearance*, Hannibal Courier-Post, April 25, 1996

Powell, Mary Jo Deney, *Letter to the Editor*, Hannibal Courier-Post, April 26, 1996

Discovered cave revives memories of lost boys, Hannibal Courier-Post, April 24, 2017

Cave biologists will map Stowell School Cave, MoDOT news release, April 25, 2006

Stowell School Cave exploration complete, MoDOT news release, April 26, 2006

Cavers give go-ahead to construction work, Quincy Herald-Whig, April 27, 2006

Boyles, Salynn, *Teens Are Hardwired for Risky Behavior*, WebMD Health News, April 13, 2007

Kolbert, Elizabeth, *The Terrible Teens; What's wrong with them?*, New Yorker magazine, August 31, 2015

Gopnik, Alison, *What's Wrong With the Teenage Mind?*, The Wall Street Journal, January 28, 2012

Divecha, Diana, *Nine Big Changes in Young Teens that You Should Know About*, developmentalscience.com/blog, February 24, 2014

Morrongiello, Barbara and Rennie, Heather, *Why Do Boys Engage in More Risk Taking Than Girls?*, Journal of Pediatric Psychology, Vol. 23, No. 1, 1998, Society of Pediatric Psychology

Balloon voyage over Cascades may be a first Seattle, Baltimore Sun, June 2, 1981
NTSB Aviation Accident Data Summary, National Transportation Safety Board May 29, 1983

Corbin, Christina, The lost boys: Mississippi River town haulted by unsolved disappearance 50 years later, Foxnews.com, May 23, 2017

John Wayne Gacy, Wikipedia, 2017

Sullivan, Terry and Maiken, Peter, *Killer Clown: the John Wayne Gacy Murders*, Pinnacle, 2011

Linedecker, Clifford, *The Man Who Killed Boys*, St. Martin's Paperbacks, 1993

About the Author

 John Wingate is a Minneapolis-based author, writer, and communications consultant. A former consumer reporter for KSTP-TV, he spent twenty years as a broadcast journalist in Illinois and Minnesota, a career path that captured his interest at age thirteen during the 1967 cave search for the lost boys of Hannibal. He has garnered nearly twenty awards for writing and reporting excellence, including three national TELLY Awards for screenwriting and video production. John was born in Hannibal, Missouri where he spent his early childhood years.

77877695R00145

Made in the USA
Lexington, KY
03 January 2018